TOGETHER for HOLY WEEK

a resource anthology

CIO PUBLISHING
Church House, Dean's Yard, Westminster SW1P 3NZ

ISBN 0 7151 0393 8

Published 1981 for the General Synod Board of Education

Printed in England by Loxley Brothers Limited, Sheffield and London

CONTENTS

FOREWORD

Together magazine has become well-known in recent years as a 'swap-shop' of ideas for all those concerned with the Christian education of children—clergy, day-school teachers, Sunday school teachers, parents. More recently still it has gained new friends through the publication of a series of anthologies of resources for Christian festivals: *Together for Christmas* and *Together Again for Christmas, Together for Festivals* and *Together for Harvest.*

No sooner did these appear than we began to receive requests from readers for yet another compilation. 'Please,' they wrote, 'can we have some ideas for Easter?' The central events of the Christian faith are more difficult to present in a form that children can cope with, and this no doubt goes far to explain the lack of such resources compared with Christmas. Here, however, is a collection that will, we hope, go some way towards meeting that need.

Its contents come from Anglican, Methodist and Roman Catholic contributors, for *Together* is ecumenical both in outlook and readership; some have been devised for use in parishes, some for day schools, and many are interchangeable, or easily adapted. All should be treated as ideas, to change as best suits your own particular group and circumstances.

If you feel that *Together* magazine, with its nine issues a year full of resources, might be of help to you, drop a line to the Circulation Manager, *Together,* Church House, Dean's Yard, Westminster, London SW1P 3NZ, for details of our subscription rates. And if you too would like to contribute ideas, write to me at the above address. 'I think I could do better than that myself' is a good fighting motto!

Pamela Egan
Editor, *Together*

THE EASTER STORY

A play for primary children, first acted in Slaughterford parish church, by Gretel Hunt

Cast:

Jesus
Pontius Pilate
Mary Magdalene
Simon Peter
Other Disciple
Crowd
Two angels
1st Person in crowd
2nd Person in crowd
3rd Person in crowd
Reader

Properties:
Stool, large cross, purple gown, crown of thorns, white linen wrappings.

Costumes:
Albs were found to be suitable for the angels.
A purple gown needs to be worn by Pontius Pilate.

SCENE 1: Jesus before Pilate

[*All children are at the back of the church. A hymn is sung by the congregation and during the last verse the Reader walks down the aisle and stands in the pulpit. When the hymn is finished the Reader reads:*]

Reader: Luke 23.1 and 2

[*When the Reader has finished, Pilate walks down the aisle and sits on the stool, which is placed in front of the altar but a little to one side. Jesus is then brought before Pilate with much pushing and shoving.*]

Crowd [*all together and with fists raised*]: Hail, Caesar!

Pilate [*to crowd*]: What wrong has this man done?

1st Person in crowd: He tells us not to pay taxes.

2nd Person in crowd: He says he will destroy the temple.

3rd Person in crowd: He says he is a king.

Pilate [*to Jesus*]: A king! Are you a king? Are you the king of the Jews?

Jesus: So you say.

Pilate [*after a pause*]: I find no fault in him.

All [*loudly and with astonishment*]: No fault in him!

1st Person in crowd: He calls himself a king!

2nd Person in crowd: He sets himself against Caesar!

All: He is worthy of death!
[*Here the crowd wave their fists in riotous fashion.*]
Crucify him, crucify him, crucify him!

Pilate: Shall I crucify your king?

All: We have no king but Caesar.
[*Then the crowd grabs Jesus. A purple robe is put on him and a crown of thorns is placed on his head. He is taken to the back of the church and the crowd laugh at him and mock him as they go. Pilate follows behind.*]

1st Person in crowd: Save yourself.

2nd Person in crowd: Who hit you?

3rd Person in crowd: So you're the king of the Jews?

SCENE 2: The Crucifixion

[*When the children are at the back of the church and all is quiet, the Reader continues:*]

Reader: John 10.16-19
[*Jesus then walks towards the altar carrying the cross. The crowd follow behind. This should be done very slowly. Jesus props the cross up in front of the altar and stands to one side, out of sight of the congregation. All others kneel before the cross, facing the altar.*]

Reader: John 19.25-30
[*At the end of this reading the children should remain while the congregation sings 'There is a green hill far away'. During the last verse, the children will stand and walk slowly to the back of the church with heads bowed. Jesus remains, but must still be hidden from the congregation.*]

SCENE 3: The Resurrection

[*The stool on which Pontius Pilate sat now becomes a tomb and the white linen wrappings are placed in front of it. The angels stand on either side of the altar. The Reader then reads:*]

Reader: Luke 21.50-56, followed by 'Early the next morning, as the new day was dawning, Mary Magdalene went out to the tomb'.
[*Mary Magdalene walks towards the tomb. The disciples follow, but remain halfway down the aisle. Mary reaches the tomb and looks cautiously inside. She steps back and then leans forward to take a second look. She gasps in surprise and horror, turns and runs breathlessly to the disciples.*]

Mary Magdalene [*to disciples*]: They have taken the Lord from the tomb and we don't know where they have put him.
[*The Other Disciple hurries to the tomb and Mary Magdalene and Simon Peter follow behind. The disciples look inside the tomb and then stand on either side of it, facing the congregation. Mary kneels in front of the tomb. The disciples hold up the linen wrappings.*]

Simon Peter and Other Disciple: It is true. See, here are the linen wrappings. We must go and tell the others.
[*They both hurry towards the back of the church. Mary starts to weep loudly. The two angels then come forward and stand on either side of the tomb. They face the congregation and hold out their arms.*]

Angels [*both together*]: Woman, why are you crying?

Mary: They have taken my Lord away and I do not know where they have put him.
[*She then continues weeping for a little while.*]

Jesus [*loudly*]: Mary, Mary.
[*Mary stands up, smiles and turns to face Jesus. She holds out her arms towards him.*]

Mary: Master.
[*Mary, Jesus and the angels stay in the same position (as statues) while the Reader reads:*]

Reader: Luke 24.25-26
[*When the Reader has finished, the congregation sings 'Jesus Christ is risen today'. The children walk in procession to the back of the church: first Jesus, then Mary, the angels and finally the Reader.*]

THE ROAD TO JERUSALEM

A puppet play for Passiontide, devised by Evelyn Ellerton for a mixed-age group of children

'The Road to Jerusalem' is a puppet play suitable for a flexible number of children of various ages.

Each child makes the puppet character which he or she will act with. It is made from a folded newspaper doubled over another roll to form a cross. This is tied to a stick and the cross firmly sellotaped. The head and arms are covered with bits of old nylon stocking secured with rubber bands. The puppet can then be dressed with scraps of material glued or sewn according to each child's ability. The tree could be real greenery and a background picture could be provided for the last scene.

SCENE 1

[*The crowd lines up in front of a tree shouting.*]

Crowd: Jesus is coming, Jesus is coming!

Zaccheus [*very small, running behind the crowd*]: Where is he, where is he? I must see Jesus. [*Climbs tree.*]

[*Jesus comes in slowly, followed by two disciples.*]

Jesus: Zaccheus, come down quickly, I am coming to stay with you today.

Crowd 1: He's a thief.

Crowd 2: He pinches our money.

Crowd 3: And Jesus is going to stay with him.

All: It's not fair!

Zaccheus: Sir, I'm not like that. Look, I'll give half my money to the poor and if I've taken too much in taxes from anyone I'll give him back four times as much.

Jesus: God himself has come to this house today. Now this man belongs to God's family too. [*He goes on, Zaccheus dancing behind him, then the disciples and the crowd.*]

SCENE 2

[*A Blind Beggar by the roadside R.*]

Beggar: Have pity on a blind man.

[*Crowd come on in twos.*]

Crowd: It's Jesus of Nazareth, Jesus of Nazareth. [*They stay behind Blind Man as Jesus enters from L.*]

Beggar [*shouting*]: Son of David, have pity on me.

Crowd 1: Shut up.

Crowd 2: Be quiet.

Crowd 3: Shhh.

Beggar: Son of David, have pity on me.

Jesus: Call him over here.

Crowd 1: Cheer up.

Crowd 2: Get up.

Crowd 3: He's calling you.

Jesus: What do you want me to do for you?

Beggar: Sir, give me back my sight.

Jesus: Go home, your trust in me has made you better. [*He goes on, the beggar dancing behind, followed by the disciples and crowd.*]

SCENE 3

[*Jesus and four disciples.*]

1: Jesus, we want to stay with you always.

2: You make sick people well.

3: You tell such wonderful stories.

4: The people want to make you their king.

1: When you are king, can I be prime minister?

All: Can we all be in your government?

Jesus: I will answer with a story and you can act it. There was once a king . . .

1: I will be king.

Jesus: And he had three servants . . .

2,3 and 4: We will be the servants.

Jesus: He called them to him and said . . . [*Jesus goes out.*]

King: I am going on a long journey, I have been made your king and now I am going away to be crowned. Here is a pound for each of you, trade with it while I am away. [*Exit.*]

2: We don't want to work for him.

3: We don't want a king who goes away.

4: Let's have fun now he's gone. [*They go off.*]

Jesus [*offstage*]: After a long time the king returned and sent for his servants. [*King comes on from one side, servants from the other.*]

King: Let me see how well you have worked for me while I have been away.

2: Your pound, sir, has made ten more.

King: Well done, you are a good servant. You shall be in charge of ten cities.

3: Your pound, sir, has made five more.

King: You shall be in charge of five cities.

4: Here is your pound, sir, I kept it safely wrapped up in my hankie.

King: You lazy good-for-nothing, take his pound and give it to the one with ten!

4: I don't like this story.

2: I wonder what it means.

3: Do you think Jesus is going away?

All: Jesus, Jesus, you aren't going away, are you?

Jesus [*entering*]: Look, we are on our way to Jerusalem. There are people there who want to kill me.

All: No, crown you!

Jesus: Kill me.

1: They can't do that.

2: It's not fair.

3: I know, we'll go to Jerusalem and you stay here.

All: Yes, you stay here. [*They go off.*]

Jesus: You will never find the King you are looking for unless you take him with you. [*Disciples come back one by one, slowly.*] We have been so happy together, but soon I must leave you. Even if they kill me it will not be the end, I will come back to you.

4: We don't understand.

1: But we'll go with you, Jesus, always.

2: Even to Jerusalem.

All: To Jerusalem!

THE KING'S TAILOR

A play for juniors
by Nigel Sustins

Narrator: There was once a Tailor whose Master was a rich and proud man. The Master never did any work, but piled it all on the Tailor, so that the unhappy man would often work very late hours to get all the jobs done.

The Tailor had a secret dream. He longed to make a really beautiful robe: something that other people would look at and admire. But his Master always bullied him, and made him work far harder than he should have worked, so that the Tailor had no time to make his beautiful robe.

One night, when the Tailor was working very late to finish off a rich lady's gown, he had a strange experience. He wasn't sure at first whether it was a dream or not. He thought that a man came into the room and spoke to him.

[*Tailor works on garment; King enters and comes up to speak to him.*]

King: Good evening, my friend, I see that you are very busy.

Tailor [*startled*]: Who's that? Oh, I didn't see you come in. Yes, I always have plenty of work to do.

King: I wondered if you could make something for me? You see, I am a King, and I would like you to make me a white robe. Nothing too gaudy or expensive, but a robe that you have put your whole heart into.

Tailor: You're a King, you say? Well, I'd like to make a robe for you. But I have so little spare time. My Master keeps me slaving away day and night. Still, I'll try my hardest. When do you want it?

King: It won't be needed for a while yet. I'll send someone to collect the robe when it's ready. Thank you.

Narrator: It seemed that the Tailor's dream was about to come true. He would make his robe—perhaps not as splendid a one as he had hoped at first, but it would be a robe to be proud of. He snatched time whenever he could to work on the robe, and often went without proper sleep so that he could add more stitches to his work.

Several weeks later, the Master told the Tailor to take a huge pile of clothes into the City to be cleaned. The Tailor set out, with clothes heaped up so high that he tottered along, and could hardly see where he was going. He came into the City, and heard shouting and singing. A large crowd was gathering near the City gate. The Tailor put down his heavy load, and sat by the road for a while to see who was coming along. Imagine his surprise when he saw a man riding a donkey, and that man was the King who had visited him and ordered the white robe.

The King's followers were running in front of him, and people were tearing down the branches of trees and laying them down on the road in front of the donkey. Some people took off their cloaks and robes and laid them out like a carpet for the King to ride over.

The Tailor was so pleased to see the King that he tugged the sleeve of one of the King's followers.

Tailor [*tugging sleeve of follower*]: Take my bundle of clothes. Lay them down in front of the King.

Narrator: The follower accepted the Tailor's offer. And so the King went on his way with the people shouting and waving their arms for joy. When the crowd had gone, the Tailor was left with his clothes to pick up. They were dirty, of course, and torn in places. However, the clothes had to be cleaned, and the Tailor staggered on with them to the laundry, as he'd intended. He hoped that the Master would not find out what he had done. The Tailor tried to complete his work on the white robe as quickly as possible. The King had arrived. He might want the robe very soon. One night, very late, the Master barged into the Tailor's room.

Master: Hey! You lazy fool! What are you doing? Leave that. I've got an important job for you.

Tailor: What do you want me to do?

Master: [*snatching the white robe*]: What's this? Doing other work, are you, when you should be doing work for me?

Tailor: [*trying to pull the robe back*]: Don't take it away! I was doing the work in my own time. It's a special robe—for a King.

Master: King? You're getting soft in the head! What kind of a King would ask you to do a job for him? I'll look after this. It looks like a good piece of work. I'll find a customer for it. Here's the job I want you to do—now! It's another robe, a purple one this time, for the Palace. Yes, the Palace! Not a King, but the next best thing. The Governor's ordered it. So get on with it!

Narrator: The Tailor was heartbroken as he saw the Master taking the white robe. He had just completed it, too. Now he had to do a job for which he had no enthusiasm at all. And suppose the King came? What would he say to him? The Tailor worked day and night on the purple robe. In the early hours of a Friday morning, the Master came into the Tailor's room.

Master: Is it finished?

Tailor: Yes, just about.

Master: Well, move your scraggy body and get the robe round to the Palace right away. The Governor wants it, urgently!

Narrator: The Tailor set off for the City with the purple robe under his arm. It was still dark. He knocked on the gate of the servants' quarters in the Palace, and someone took him down a winding passage. He heard the sound of laughter and shouting, and as he came out into a courtyard he saw the Governor's soldiers standing together in a crowd. They were making fun of someone. Imagine the Tailor's horror when he saw the King. The soldiers had beaten him, and he stood there with his head bowed.

Soldier 1: He thinks he's a King. Silly dreamer!

Soldier 2: Why don't we give him a crown? Here, I'll make one for him.

[*Soldier twists together sprigs of thorns to make a crown, and puts it on King's head.*]

Soldier 2: There we are. Sorry that the edges of your crown are rather sharp, King!

Soldier 3: He needs a King's robe too. [*Sees Tailor*] Hey, you—what's that under your arm?

Tailor: It's something for the Governor, a special order.

Soldier 3: Looks just right for this King here. [*Grabs robe and holds it up to examine it*] Well, bless me! It's a King's robe all right. Here, King. Try this for size.

[*Soldier drapes robe over King's shoulders.*]

Soldier 1: Doesn't he look lovely?

[*They all laugh.*]

Narrator: The Tailor went home feeling very sad. His King would never come for the white robe now, even if he'd still had it to give him. News came to the Tailor of what was happening in the City. The King was taken out to a hillside, and hung up on a wooden cross. He was killed as if he had been a criminal.

The Master came into the Tailor's room in the evening.

Master: What an exciting day! You missed all the fun. A really good execution, it was. The poor devil didn't last long. He was worn out with all the beating he'd had. Oh, by the way, I've sold your white robe.

Tailor: What?

Master: I said, I've sold your white robe. A very good customer. Very wealthy. He paid a good price.

Narrator: The Tailor was more unhappy than he had ever been before.

He sat in his room all day Saturday (even his Master let him have a day of rest) and he brooded about the King who was dead, and the loss of the white robe. In the evening, he had a visitor.

Stranger: Good evening, Tailor.

Tailor: Good evening, Sir. What can I do for you?

Stranger: I thought you'd like to know that the King is now in need of the robe you made for him.

Tailor: But haven't you heard the news? The King is dead. And besides, I haven't got the robe. My Master sold it.

Stranger: I know. He sold it to me. I am about to take the King his robe. He has been lying on a cold stone slab, wrapped only in strips of cloth, and covered by a death-sheet. Now, he is about to prove himself a King. He will prove himself a mighty man, who conquers his enemies. What is the greatest enemy of mankind?

Tailor: I don't know—fear? Unhappiness?

Stranger: Death is a greater enemy. Our King will defeat death.

Tailor: But how? I don't understand what you're saying.

Stranger: It is enough that you understand this. The King will rise from his slab; he will leave behind him the strips of cloth and the sheet. And as he comes out of the tomb he will need your robe. The one you made especially for him. Give thanks to God! I speak the truth.

Narrator: The Tailor was filled with a sudden joy. Could it be possible? Could the King come alive again? In the days to come, the news would spread through the City; the King who died on the criminal's cross has been seen again—alive!

The Tailor left his bullying Master, and joined the King's followers. He travelled with them, mending their clothes and making new ones. And when the King met all his followers on a hill, and told them that he must go away to his real Kingdom, the Tailor nearly wept with joy to see what the King was wearing: the white robe he had made.

THE MYSTERY OF THE THREE MARIES AND OF MARY MAGDALENE AND THE APOSTLES

Isobel Galilee's free adaptation of two old Cornish 'mystery' plays was originally presented by children of 8-10, but it would also suit an older or mixed age group

[*Enter Mary Magdalene, Mary the mother of James, and Mary Salome.*]

Mary M: What shall we do?
Today is the third day
Since my Lord went into the tomb.

Mary, m. of James: He was of great comfort to us,
Yet we had to see him die.

Mary Salome: We must go and see if the body of Christ
is risen as he said to us.

Mary M: O let us hurry at once
For the stone is raised from the tomb.

Mary, m. of James: We have stayed away too long.
He's been taken away from the tomb.
Now we'll never see him again.

Mary Salome: I believe that he is risen up on this very day.
But what will happen if we do not find him?

1st Angel: I know who you are looking for.
Jesus is not here,
For he is risen to life.

Mary M: O angel, tell me where he has gone.
It would make me so joyful to see him once again.

2nd Angel: Mary, go and say to his disciples and Peter
He is going to meet them in Galilee,
Just as he promised them.

Mary, m. of James: Now he is risen again indeed,
Jesus our Saviour.
He is lord of heaven and earth.

Mary Salome: Let us go to the city
And tell everyone what we have seen,
That Jesus is risen.

Mary M: I won't go to the city unless I find him.
I want to see him once again.

Mary, m. of James & Mary Salome: May God bless you.

[*They go out*]

Mary M: [*facing audience*] Christ, hear my voice and give me grace
To meet with you and see your face.

[*Enter Jesus, behind her*]

Jesus: Why are you so sad?

Mary M: [*turning round*] Good Sir, if you have chanced to see
Christ my Saviour, tell me where he is.

Jesus: Mary, would you know him
If you saw him before you?

Mary M: I know Jesus the Son of Mary well,
But I can't see him anywhere.
That is why I am so sad.

Jesus: Mary, see my five wounds.
Believe me truly to be risen from the dead.

Mary M: [*kneels*] You are our Master . . .

Jesus: Do not touch me.
But go and tell my disciples
I am going into Galilee.

[*Jesus goes out. Mary Magdalene watches him go, with her back to the audience. Enter eleven disciples.*]

Mary M: [*turning round*] O disciples, I have good news for you.
Jesus is risen from the dead.
I've just seen him: I spoke to him too.

Thomas: Silence, woman, with your tales.
Speak the truth.
I won't believe that Christ who was so cruelly
Killed is alive.

Mary M: I'm speaking the truth, Thomas.
I saw him just now.
He sent me here to tell you.

Thomas: Silence, don't mock us!
If you do, I could hit you.

Mary M: I won't be silent through fear.
I'll prove it before I go.

Peter: Why, Thomas, I'm full of joy
To hear that Christ is risen.

Thomas: Peter, be quiet.
It is idle to say that Christ is risen.
A man can't be raised after dying.

James: Thomas, it may be true.
Jesus was the Son of God.
He made heaven and earth.
He could rise again if he wanted.

Thomas: O James, it's a waste of time
To say things like that.
A man who is dead doesn't live again.

John: Thomas, you're a fool.
Jesus told us all that after dying
He would rise again after three days.

Thomas: John, don't be silly.
Christ suffered and died on the cross.
Curse them that did it!

Bartholomew: Thomas, believe me though I am old and grey.
Men could not have the power to put him to death.
He died for us, to rise
And carry all Christians to heaven.

Thomas: O Barty, you're mad.
God could have saved everyone without *dying.*

Matthew: That is true.
But he could have destroyed everything too.
Christ chose to go into the tomb
And to live again.

Thomas: And you're a fool, Matthew.
He's dead, in spite of all you say.
I saw him dead on the Cross.

Andrew: Thomas, be quiet.
Surely our Lord is risen again.
For Mary spoke to him.

Thomas: You've been taken in, Andrew.
The girl has told a lie.
I won't believe it as long as I live.

Mary M: I haven't said an untrue word!
He showed me his wounds.
Mary, Mother of James, and Mary Salome
Will bear witness to what I say.

Thomas: Hold your tongue!
God help me, I don't like lies.

[*Enter Jesus from behind*]

Jesus: The peace of God be with you all.

[*Disciples slowly kneel, Thomas last*]

Thomas: My Lord and my God.

NOTES

1. Jesus and the angels were concealed by sitting them at the far end of the choir stalls from where they could enter and to which they returned. Other characters entered from the nave or side aisles.

2. Most churches have angel costumes for Christmas plays. Our angels wore these and the Maries wore plain white gowns and blue head coverings. Jesus wore a white robe and a medieval-looking halo.

The disciples were asked to wear one of Dad's shirts, belted over shorts and sandals (no headgear). The result was a reasonable compromise between 'biblical' and medieval and had a timeless quality which suited the play.

3. Our choir provided a musical framework by singing verses from a medieval Easter carol at the beginning, while the disciples entered, and at the end of the play. The final 'tableau' of Jesus and the kneeling disciples was 'frozen' while the verse was sung.

Suitable carols might be 'The Sans Day Carol' *(Oxford Book of Carols)* or 'The World itself keeps Easter Day' *(Oxford Book of Carols),* with verses 1 and 2 sung at the beginning, 3 and 4 in the middle and verse 5 at the end.

'I DIDN'T KNOW . . .'

An Easter play for over 10s
by Margery Robinson

Across the back of the stage runs a wall which ends in an opening on the extreme right leading to a Youth Club Hall. The wall need only be painted cardboard. No actual door is necessary, although as members enter there should be the sounds of a door opening and closing. A disco is in progress; as the door opens bursts of music and voices come through. All the characters are casually dressed for a disco evening.

Characters:

Jenny (a 12-year old)

Claire (a little older, friend of Trina)

Katrina (called Trina, an Irish girl now living here)

Cathy (older than the rest, an obvious leader)

Tracy (also a 12-year old)

Graham (Cathy's special friend)

Jim (a club member about the same age)

David (youth leader about 30)

[*A number of club members pass at intervals to go into the hall: they exchange greetings with the knot of members outside.*]

SCENE 1

[*Outside entrance to hall. All enter from left to right. Jenny enters, pauses by the entrance, then waves to Claire who has just entered.*]

Jenny: Seen Cathy? She's late!

Claire: Miss Thomas gave her a detention. She tore up Trina's English book. I saw her although she denied it.

Tracey [*joining them*]: Coming? [*She starts to go in.*]

Jenny: We're waiting for Cathy. [*Two or three members pass and enter.*]

Tracey: She won't mind if we go in. [*There is a burst of music and laughter.*] It's started. Come on.

Claire [*firmly*]: I must wait.

Jenny [*astonished*]: You don't mean . . .

Tracey: You've invited Trina, haven't you?

Claire: Yes I have. Trina's my best friend. I don't care *where* she's from. She's the nicest girl I know.

Tracey: I agree, but it's sure to cause a scene with Cathy.

Jenny: She's always so quiet. I like her too, but even her name sends Cathy into a frenzy.

Tracey: Look how furious she was when David gave Trina a part in the Easter play. I thought she was going to tear up the script.

Claire: I don't know why she was so mad. She's got the best part.

Jenny [*loyally*]: Cathy's a jolly good actress.

[*Several members pass the group and go in except Jim who joins the group. A sound of music and voices are heard. The door closes.*]

Jim: Waiting for me? [*Laughingly he bows and offers each arm.*] Why so serious? I thought this was to be a jolly evening.

Cathy [*breathless from running*]: Glad you waited for me. How do I look?

[*She opens her coat and twirls round, displaying a new trouser suit.*] Like it?

Jenny: It's terrific. Have you put some make-up on?

Cathy: A little of Mum's. Does it show much?

Tracey: I'll say. Let's go in. [*They all troop towards the entrance except Claire.*]

Cathy [*impatiently)*: Come on, Claire.

Claire: I'm waiting for Trina.

Cathy [*suddenly exploding*]: How could you spoil the evening? Fancy inviting her after all her lot's done to me.

Claire: She can't help the terrorists. It's not her fault she's Irish.

Cathy: Then why is she over here? We don't want her kind.

Claire: She's staying with her aunt for a while, my Mum says.

Jim: Can't think why you make such a scene, Cathy. She's a nice girl. Pretty, too.

Cathy [*furiously*]: That's typical. You've no loyalty, that's your trouble. A pretty face and you forget everything.

Jim [*amused*]: Come off it, Cathy. Who am I supposed to be loyal to?

Cathy: To all our troops fighting over there against her lot.

Claire: I don't understand you. Just mention Ireland and you go almost mad.

Jim: There are good and bad people there same as here, so why pick on Trina?

Cathy: Because her lot killed my Uncle Bill. It was his first year in the army, only been there a few months. That lot sent a bullet right through him. I'll *never* forgive them. He was such fun. Saving up for a sports car he was. My Mum was saving his money for him. [*She turns away to wipe her eyes.*] Now he'll never need one. He was my Mum's little brother. She misses him something awful. Every night I hear her crying through the wall.

[*Trina comes along. Claire hurries to meet her. She takes her arm.*]

Trina [*timidly*]: Hullo there.

Jim [*warmly*]: Hullo Trina. I was just going in.

[*He joins Claire and Trina, they all disappear into the hall. Cathy makes a face behind Trina's back. There is a burst of music as the door opens and closes.*]

Jenny: Come on, we're missing all the fun.

[*Jenny and Tracey start to go in but Cathy hangs back.*]

Cathy [*fastening her coat*]: I'm going home. She spoilt my whole evening. I'd rather go back than be on the same floor with her.

Tracey: But you share the same classroom.

Cathy [*fiercely*]: I can't help that, my Mother won't let me leave, but I'll not go near her unless I must.

[*She walks slowly off the way she came, but meets Graham halfway along. Jenny and Tracey, with a backward glance, go into the hall.*]

Graham: Sorry I'm late but I couldn't get my homework done. Could have finished it tomorrow, but I like the weekend free. What's the matter?

Cathy: I'm not coming.

Graham: Why? You look super. [*There is a long silence as Cathy studies the ground.*] You're not still on about Trina, are you? You've done everything to make her life a misery at school. You've ganged up against her, influenced that stupid Williams boy to pull her hair. What's she ever done to you? Nothing! Forget it and come along, for my sake.

Cathy: No, I can't.

Graham: I thought we were special friends, but not any more. I can't think why David put you in the Easter Play. He should have given your part to Trina, she's only got a tiny part. Cathy, you make me sick! [*He walks off and enters the hall.*]

Cathy [*desperately*]: Graham, come back, I . . .

[*David enters, carrying some records. He goes up to Cathy who is crying bitterly.*]

David: What's happened? Why are you so upset?

Cathy [*gulping down her tears*]: It's . . . Trina . . . Everyone says I've been dreadful to her, but nobody sees it from my side.

David: Suppose you tell me your side.

Cathy: You see, it was losing my Uncle Bill. Mum, Susan and I have only got each other, having no Father, and Uncle Bill always stayed with us on leave. I loved him so much. He was like the brother I never had. Then Trina's lot shot him just as he was coming home on leave the next day. [*Fiercely*] How I hate 'em all.

David: When there's a war, people who have nothing to do with it get hurt. Good folk, kind, loving people all suffer. You mustn't hate anyone, you're adding to the war if you do.

Cathy: I don't see that.

David: Today the world is a very dark place, wars, killings, hunger, homelessness, refugees being pushed from one place to another. Each of us carries a small torch; anger, greed, hatred and selfishness switch off the light, but friendship, kindness and particularly love turn on the light with an ever-increasing beam. We need as many lit torches as we can get. Cathy, your light has gone out, so you're adding to the darkness.

Cathy: All I know is that I hate Trina and her lot. Anyway, what is she doing over here?

David: I promised Trina's aunt I wouldn't tell her story. I can see I shall have to.

Cathy [*impatiently*]: Go on then.

David: Trina lived with her parents and younger sister in Ulster. One Saturday just before Christmas, they set off to do some shopping leaving Trina at home with a bad cold. On the way back they were caught in crossfire between our troops and the terrorists. The army shouted at them to go back but either they never heard or were too scared to move. When the firing stopped they were all dead on the pavement.

Cathy [*slowly, trying to take it all in*]: You mean one of our soldiers could have fired those bullets. [*In horror*] It could have been . . .

David: It was crossfire. They were caught in the middle.

Cathy [*hysterically*]: I don't believe it. You're trying to scare me.

David: I'm telling you just how badly Trina has been hurt. She has no one but her aunt.

Cathy: . . . and I made things far worse for her. Why didn't you tell me? I didn't know.

David: Go home and think about it. You need her forgiveness.

Cathy [*in great distress*]: I didn't know. I didn't know.

SCENE 2

[*The stage is set for the Easter Morning Story. Jim and Graham (dressed in overalls) are moving the props. These are very simple. An aperture, to represent the tomb. A torch which can be switched on from without. Bands of linen laid inside the tomb. A large object for the stone. A tree and shrubs, but these are not necessary. An overhead light capable of becoming brighter. As the boys work they talk.*]

Jim: What shall we do if Cathy doesn't come?

Graham: Don't know. I don't think she'll let us down.

Jim: She hasn't been to school for ten days. No one has seen her since the disco.

Graham: I feel it's partly my fault. I told her I didn't know why she had a part in the Easter Play. I hadn't any right to say that.

Jim: She asked for it. [*He moves a prop.*] Remember David said that if we all thought kindly of Cathy she'd respond. Love always works, he said. Some joke. Cathy's let us down.

Graham: I've been thinking about that all the weekend. But isn't this play about people who wanted proof?

Jim: I like proof. I shan't believe any of David's talk until I see people made different with my own eyes.

Graham: Seems to me that you should have been called Thomas. [*Someone beckons from the wings. He goes off and returns immediately.*] David says Cathy's come. We're to hurry.

[*They finish setting the stage and go off.*]

The Easter Play

Mary Magdalene is played by Cathy

Peter is played by Jim

John is played by Graham

Mary (Mother of Jesus) is played by Claire

Mary (Mother of James) is played by Trina

Jesus is played by David

[*The play is a mimed presentation of the Easter morning story, with a Narrator reading the Bible account. It reaches the point when Mary Magdalene has come to visit the tomb. She carries a small jar. She enters from the left and wanders around, looking everwhere. She stands weeping by the tomb, then returns to the left-hand corner of the stage. She fails to see Jesus at first who has entered from the right. Looking up she hurries towards him.*]

Mary: Please, sir, they have taken away the body of Jesus and I don't know where he is. Have you seen where they have taken him?

Jesus: Mary. [*He stretches out a hand. The overhead light beams down so that he stands a figure of light.*]

Mary: Master. [*Then, dropping to her knees, she starts to weep. Her need for forgiveness is so real and urgent that she feels in the actual presence of the Master.*] Master, I have done dreadful things . . . I have hurt Trina . . . led others to be cruel to her. My heart's been full of hate . . . I'm so sorry but I didn't know . . . I did love my Uncle Bill so much, and Trina must have loved her family even more. Now war has taken them all away . . . and I've added to it. I can't expect Trina to forgive me, she wouldn't and I don't blame her, but will you forgive me? Will you, Master?

Jesus [*full of compassion*]: Cathy. [*Both his hands are now outstretched in blessing. Quietly from the wings Trina slips in and kneels beside Cathy. The light now brightens and shines on both girl's bowed heads.*

[*Either an unseen choir or the whole congregation sings 'Jesus, good above all other'. The girls remain kneeling, receiving the blessing, until the end of the hymn.*]

CHRIST IS ALIVE!

a modern Passion Play.
Roy Kirk describes a successful group enterprise.

It is always very difficult to describe successfully to children the meaning and significance of Good Friday and all that led up to and immediately followed it—the triumph of the entry into Jerusalem on Palm Sunday, the turn of fortunes during the following week, the tragedy of Good Friday itself and the utter joy of the unbelievable happening of Easter morning. One Easter, at St. Mary's Church, Humberstone, we decided to try and describe the Easter story in as vivid a way as possible by acting out the modern Passion Play detailed below during a Sunday school session.

We intended to involve all the Sunday school children (about 40 at that time) either in individual parts, or in 'crowd scenes', with the specific aim of giving them a 'feel' of that first Holy Week. We wanted to use the minimum of 'props' and the only major item of equipment needed was a cross made from a bamboo rod from the centre of a roll of carpet and a piece of hardboard, which formed the horizontal arm. This was light enough for a child to drag along, but large enough to give the impression of the size of the original cross.

The play was purposely written so that it could be tape-recorded (in the absence of filming or video-recording facilities) and this we did as the action went along. Later, music was added to the beginning and end of the tape, in addition to a radio-play-type introduction, resulting in a useful audio-aid which can be used again and again for teaching and other purposes. For example, the tape was played during an exhibition in the Church Hall in June when the work of the Sunday school during the previous year was on display.

We would recommend that two teachers—or perhaps two very senior children—play the parts of News Reader and Radio Reporter, as these are 'anchor roles' which set the scenes throughout the action of the play. We were lucky enough to have found some slides of the Oberammergau Passion Plays and we showed these to the children before we enacted the play, to see what realism can really be captured. Of one thing we are sure—an enjoyable time was had by everyone, especially during the 'crowd scenes', and the end result was a deeper understanding of the meaning of Easter.

One footnote: we hope to perform the play at one of our monthly half-hour Family Services, as close to Easter as possible, of course.

Again, the minimum amount of equipment needed (although costumes could be worn if necessary) and the running commentaries throughout the play, eliminating the need for scenery, make it an ideal play for such a service. Different parts of the church can be used for particular scenes; the central aisle makes a ready-made street in Jerusalem for the crowd sequences, while the News Reader can stand in the pulpit for his, or her, broadcasts.

We hope that other Sunday schools and similar groups will find this as stimulating a way of explaining Easter as we did.

The main individual parts:

Jesus	Chief Priest
Judas	2 ladies
2 soldiers	News Reader
Pontius Pilate	Radio Reporter

[*In addition eleven additional children will be needed to play the parts of disciples in the Last Supper scene and all the children present will be needed to form crowds at the appropriate points in the play.*]

[*A News Reader sits at a table at one end of the room, or hall, and remains there, reading the news, for the whole of the play*].

News Reader: Good morning. This is Palestine Radio. Here is the 10 a.m. news for Sunday [*insert appropriate Holy Week date here.*] . News has just come through that the man known as Jesus and his followers, whom he calls his disciples, have appeared at the gates of Jerusalem. All week reports have been coming in of their journey from Galilee along the valley of the River Jordan. We will go over immediately to our man on the spot.

[*A Radio Reporter stands at the opposite end of the room, or hall.*]

Radio Reporter: I am standing at the North Gate of the city with a vast crowd of people which seems to grow in size every minute. The noise they are making is tremendous and the excitement and joy very intense. Wait a moment . . . here comes Jesus now: he seems to have obtained a donkey from somewhere and he is riding into the city to a glorious welcome. Just listen to the cheering . . .

[*During the report all the children form two lines for Jesus to walk between. As Jesus moves away from the Radio Reporter towards the opposite end of the room, or hall, between the two lines all the children begin to cheer and shout. Some shout 'Hosanna', others 'Blessed is the King' and as Jesus moves amongst the crowd so they begin to follow him. The noise gradually dies down as Jesus reaches the other end of the room, or hall.*]

Radio Reporter: The procession has now moved on to the city of Jerusalem, leaving behind an atmosphere of jubilation and the roads strewn with clothes and palm leaves. The people of Jerusalem feel, obviously, that this man Jesus is about to bring about great changes for them. We will do our best to keep you informed of future events in these exciting times. Meanwhile, back to the studio . . .

News Reader: Good evening. Here is the 9 p.m. news for Thursday [*insert date*]. We have further news of the man Jesus, whom we saw enter the city of Jerusalem at first hand last Sunday. Regular listeners will know that Jesus has made enemies of the Chief Priests and Scribes, first by chasing the money-lenders out of the Temple and, on the following day, by making them look foolish in their answers to his questions. It is clear that they would like to see him tried and executed, but people still think of him as King. Yesterday they flocked to the Temple to hear him proclaim—and here we quote—that he was 'a light come into the World so that all who have faith in me shall not be left in darkness'. Today, of course, is the Feast of the Passover and we have a radio van outside the house where Jesus and his followers are to celebrate the Feast. Let us go over to our reporter now.

[*The Radio Reporter stands in another part of the room, or hall. Near to him Jesus and the twelve disciples are seated at a table with Jesus in the middle.*]

Radio Reporter: I am sitting outside the house and Jesus and his disciples have just entered ready for the Feast.

Jesus: I want you to take this bread and eat and then to drink this wine. Please do this always and remember me. Always love one another so that everyone will know that you believe in me and still follow me, even when I am dead. Yes . . . I will soon die and I have something serious to say to two of you in particular. One of you will betray me to the Chief Priests, while you, my faithful Peter, will deny that you ever knew me—not once, but three times. But now, Peter I will wash your feet as a mark of my love for you.
[*Jesus stoops to wash Peter's feet while Judas slips away from the table, moves past the Radio Reporter to another part of the room, or hall.*]

Radio Reporter: We have some dramatic news to bring to our listeners. Not five minutes ago a man was seen to leave the house where Jesus and his followers were celebrating the Feast of the Passover and he has run quickly towards the guardhouse. Meanwhile, Jesus himself is just leaving the house and seems to be going towards the Garden of Gethsemane. Our radio car will follow him there . . .

[*Jesus leaves the disciples and the table, moves to another part of the room, or hall (followed by the Radio Reporter) and kneels down in prayer.*]

Radio Reporter: As we thought, Jesus has come to the Garden of Gethsemane and is kneeling in prayer at this moment. But wait . . . seemingly unbeknown to him two Roman soldiers are being led in his direction.
[*Judas and two soldiers appear near to the Radio Reporter.*]

Judas: There he is—just over there.

Soldier: Go and point him out clearly to us.

[*Judas goes over and kisses Jesus. He then runs away past the Radio Reporter and the two soldiers arrest Jesus and hustle him away.*]

Radio Reporter: The soldiers have now arrested Jesus and they are leading him away to jail. The man who pointed him out to the soldiers has run off, but as he passed our radio car it looked very much like the disciple known as Judas. We will now return you to the newsroom . . .

News Reader: Good morning. Here is the 7 a.m. news for Friday [*insert date*]. There has been a dramatic change in the events which we have been following all this week. Arrested last night, the man called Jesus was tried by the Chief Priests and found guilty of blasphemy because he insisted that he was the Son of God. He was sentenced to death, but the only man who has power to confirm the sentence is Pontius Pilate, the Roman Governor. Jesus is due to appear before him now and our radio car is at the scene. . .

[*The Radio Reporter stands at the opposite end of the room, or hall. Pontius Pilate sits in a chair with Jesus standing before him, the latter flanked by two soldiers. A Chief Priest stands to one side of the two facing men.*]

Radio Reporter: I am standing outside the Courtroom with a very large crowd, even though it is only just turned 7 o'clock in the morning. Jesus has just been taken into No. 1 Court and we have managed to put a microphone in the chamber to listen to the trial.

Pontius Pilate: I do not find any fault in this man. He is innocent of any charge you have brought against him. In my opinion you are afraid of this man and want to rid yourselves of him.

Chief Priest: We are certainly not afraid of this man—but remember, if you do not condemn this man to death we will inform Rome that you are a traitor to the Roman Empire. This man is a danger to Rome, not us.

Pontius Pilate: Very well, the decision is yours. I wash my hands of him. Take him away to be crucified!

[*Jesus is led away by the soldiers to one end of the room, or hall.*]

Radio Reporter: I have moved away from the Courtroom and we are nearly outside the city gate at the foot of Calvary Hill. The jeers of the crowd—that very same crowd that cheered Jesus last Sunday—can be heard quite plainly as Jesus drags his own cross on the way to his death by crucifixion. He has just come into sight . . . listen to those jeering people . . .

[*All the children form two lines again, this time booing and jeering and shouting 'Crucify him' over and over again. Jesus, dragging his cross, slowly moves through the crowd. Whenever he stumbles the soldiers who accompany him whip him. On reaching the end of the room, or hall, the cross is raised against a chair and Jesus stands on this with arms outstretched against the cross as though crucified.*]

News Reader: Good morning. Here is the 9 a.m. news for Sunday [*insert date*]. It is now two days since Jesus died on the cross and his body was temporarily put into a nearby cave. Today they are to bury him properly and we have our reporter at the cave to describe the scene.

[*The Radio Reporter stands at the other end of the room, or hall, with two very excited girls.*]

Radio Reporter: You have just come over at a very astonishing moment. We have some amazing, exciting and very wonderful news. I have with me two ladies who went to the cave early this morning ready to anoint the body of Jesus. Let them tell you in their own words what they saw . . .

First Lady: Mary and I went to the cave and found the huge stone that twenty of us had rolled over the entrance moved back.

Second Lady: Yes, and standing there was an angel who told us the unbelievable news that Jesus was alive again.

First Lady: She ran to tell the men who were coming to the cave and I ran into Jesus himself walking through the garden. It is as he always said—that he would rise again after his death.

Second Lady: Yes, we must dash off to tell the others in the city . . .

[*The two girls dash off excitedly.*]

Radio Reporter: Thank you very much. This has indeed been a day to remember. Jesus has come alive again. Already we can hear the joyful shouting of voices in the city as the news spreads amongst his supporters. There is a definite feeling of optimism in the air, already, as I return you to the studio . . .

THE GOOD FRIDAY NARRATIVE

A straightforward dramatisation by G. Calcott, suitable for reading, assembly or service.

Narrator: Pilate, the Roman Governor, ordered Jesus to be beaten, and the soldiers opened his back with the leaded whip; and they made a crown of thorns and placed it on his head and robed him in royal purple. And they mocked him, saying—

Soldiers: Hail, King of the Jews! Hail, King of the Jews!

Narrator: And they struck him with their fists. Pilate went outside again and said to the Jews—

Pilate: I am going to bring him out to you now, but understand clearly that I find him Not Guilty.

Narrator: Then Jesus came out wearing the crown of thorns and the purple robe. And Pilate said—

Pilate: Behold the man!

Narrator: At sight of him the chief priests and the Jewish officials began yelling—

All: Crucify! Crucify!

Pilate: You crucify him. I find him not guilty.

All: By our laws he ought to die. [*One voice*] Yes, he ought to die because he called himself the Son of God. [*All*] Crucify, crucify.

Narrator: When Pilate heard this, he was more frightened than ever. He took Jesus back into the palace again and asked him—

Pilate: Where are you from?

Narrator: But Jesus gave no answer.

Pilate: You won't talk to me. Don't you realise that I have the power to release you or to crucify you?

Narrator: Then Jesus said—

Jesus: You would have no power at all over me unless it were given to you from above. So those who brought me to you have the greater sin.

Narrator: Then Pilate tried to release him, but the Jewish leaders told him—

A Leader: If you release this man, you are no friend of Caesar's. Anyone who declares himself a king is a rebel against Caesar.

All: Crucify him! Crucify him!

Narrator: At these words Pilate brought Jesus out to them again and sat down at the Judgement bench. He said to the Jews—

Pilate: Here is your King!

All: Away with him, away with him—crucify him!

Pilate: What, crucify your King?

A Leader: We have no King but Caesar.

All: Crucify him, crucify him.

Narrator: So they had him at last, and he was taken out of the city, carrying his cross to the place known as the Skull. There they crucified him, and two others with him, one on either side. And Pilate posted a sign over him reading—

Pilate [*pointing*]: JESUS of NAZARETH, the KING of the JEWS.

Narrator: And the chief priests and Jewish leaders also mocked him.

1st Person: He saved others, himself he cannot save.

2nd Person: So you are the King of Israel, are you? Come down from the cross and we'll believe you.

Narrator: That afternoon, the whole earth was covered with darkness for three hours, from noon until three o'clock. About three o'clock, Jesus shouted—

Jesus: My God, my God, why have you forsaken me?

Narrator: He then bowed his head and said—

Jesus: [*slowly and deliberately*] It is finished.

Narrator: And so he died.

CHRISTIANS ON TRIAL

Janet Green found that a document from the early Church made a deep impression upon a Bristol boys' school

I have used a number of Assemblies recently where the germ of the idea came from items in *Together.* By way of a 'thank you' I thought you might like the following transcript of a genuine trial which took place in North Africa in AD 180. Ours is a secondary school (all boys) and I found that they, as an audience, were very moved by the reading. I acted as narrator, reading all the tricky names and including the bits that usually are omitted in readings, 'Speratus said', 'Cittinus said', etc. We felt that by including these we would add to the official sound of the proceedings. We made no attempt to dress up or act; we felt that the words spoke for themselves.

The cast were impressed by the obvious sincerity of the proconsul, who was bending over backwards to try and make these Christians see reason. He was clearly baffled by the situation. I waited till after the reading to point out that the names suggest to us that some of the accused were women; schools with boys and girls won't have that problem. 'I'm glad you didn't change their names,' said one of the boys afterwards, despite the fact that he had read Vestia's line. I found that they had all identified very strongly with these Christians.

The reason that had prompted me to choose this reading was the fact that the boys had just been given Gideon New Testaments, so the Bible was the 'in' thing of the moment. At the end of the reading I drew their attention to the reference to the letters of Paul, to remind them that the New Testament has a living history. I was in the fortunate position of being able to follow this theme through all the school RE lessons that week, but I see the trial transcript as a useful launching point for many themes: the sign of the fish; persecution, from the story of St. Alban to the present day; how the keeping of the first day of the week became an easy means of identifying Christians, for proconsuls as baffled as this one. For teachers who want a more secular theme: the significant point to which this reading gives life is the fact that there was once a time when one's religion was not a matter of convention and in no way second-hand, but a matter of life and death.

Note for historical enthusiasts: AD 180 was the year in which the Emperor Marcus Aurelius died.

THE TRIAL OF THE SCILLITAN CHRISTIANS, NORTH AFRICA, AD 180

(Official transcript of the trial)

Narrator: On the seventeenth day of July, at Carthage, there were brought before the court: Speratus, Nartzalus, Cittinus, Donata, Secunda, Vestia and others. Saturninus the proconsul conducted the trial.

Saturninus the proconsul said: By the mercy of the Emperor you can go free from this court: IF you return to your senses.

Speratus said: We have never done any wrong, we have not committed any crime, we have never even spoken ill, in fact, even when punished for nothing we have given thanks. That is because we are loyal to the Emperor—*our* Emperor.

Saturninus the proconsul said: I don't see what the problem is. We are very tolerant to religious people. We too are very religious. Our religion is simple. All we want you to do is to swear by the greatness of our Lord the Emperor and pray for his welfare. We do it; you ought to do so too.

Speratus said: If you will just listen, I'll explain to you the mysteries of our belief; they too are simple.

Saturninus said: I will not listen if you intend to speak evil against our traditions. All I want to hear is an oath from you in the name of the Emperor of the Roman World.

Speratus said: The empire of this world I know not; but rather I serve that God whom no man hath seen nor with these eyes can see. I have committed no theft; in fact, if I buy anything I pay the tax. I am a responsible citizen because I know my Lord, the King of Kings and the Emperor of all nations.

Saturninus the proconsul said to the rest of the accused: At least the rest of you don't be obstinate. Cease to be of this criminal persuasion.

Speratus said: Are you persuading us to break the law of the land by telling a lie?

Saturninus the proconsul said: I'm asking you to stop this foolishness for your own sakes.

Cittinus said: We have nothing to fear, except letting down our Lord God who is in heaven.

Donata said: Honour belongs to Caesar as Caesar, but our first loyalty is to God.

Vestia said: I am a Christian too.

Secunda said: I am a Christian and I don't want to be anything else.

Saturninus the proconsul said to Speratus: Do you persist in being a Christian?

Speratus said: I am a Christian.
[*And with him they all agreed.*]

Saturninus the proconsul said: Do you want some time to think about it?

Speratus said: There's nothing to think about; it's so straightforward that there's no need.

Saturninus the proconsul said: What are the things in that box you have with you?

Speratus said: Just some books.

Saturninus the proconsul said: Are they magic spells?

Speratus said: No, they are just copies of letters from Paul; a just man.

Saturninus the proconsul said: I'll give you one last chance: have a delay of thirty days to think it out.

Speratus said a second time: I've told you; I'm a Christian.
There will be no changing of my mind.

[*And with him they all agreed.*]

Saturninus the proconsul read out the decree from the tablet concerning Speratus, Nartzalus, Cittinus, Donata, Vestia, Secunda and the rest:

Having confessed that they live according to the Christian way, and after being offered the opportunity of returning to the custom of the Romans, having continued to persist obstinately in their belief, it is determined that they be put to the sword.

Speratus said: We give thanks to God.

Nartzalus said: Today we are martyrs in heaven; thanks be to God.

[*Saturninus the proconsul ordered it to be declared to the herald:*]

Speratus, Nartzalus, Cittinus, Veturius, Felix, Aquilinus, Laetantius, Januaria, Generosa, Vestia, Donata and Secunda, I have ordered to be executed.

Those sentenced all said: Thanks be to God.

DARKNESS AND LIGHT

Easter plays can range from the simple to the elaborate. Jenny Tingle describes a full-scale production using drama, dance, lighting and sound effects and involving parishioners of all ages, which was performed in her Stanmore church to great effect.

Background

When a group of people from St. Anselm's Church, Belmont, Harrow decided to write and perform a play in church, it was originally intended to invite all the children and young people connected with the church to participate. As the idea was discussed, the production became more and more ambitious. The theme of Darkness and Light was chosen and as all possibilities were explored it was realised that it would need all ages and a great many varying talents to bring it about. A team of interested and talented people were assembled—a writer, producer, stage manager, props., as well as people specially talented in lighting, sound production, costumes, music etc. A general invitation was issued to anyone interested to take part and in the event the age range of actors was from six months (Jesus as a baby) to 78 years ('Simeon'). The majority were young people from the Sunday schools and youth organisations, but the adults of the congregation assisted with the 'voices' on tape and narration.

St. Anselm's Church is very large and lofty so, in order that everything could be heard well, it was decided to tape everything beforehand and merely to mime it all on the day. The sound was relayed through the church's amplification system, with some additional equipment. Rehearsals, held in church on Sunday afternoons, lasted for some seven weeks. Costumes were fitted and made during this time and as soon as a costume was finished that character wore it at least once, so that by the time the final rehearsal came everyone was used to his robes.

The first rehearsals were, of course, to get the actions right. As soon as possible it was necessary to have the music available and the taped voices ready so that actors could get used to the timing and interpretation of the music.

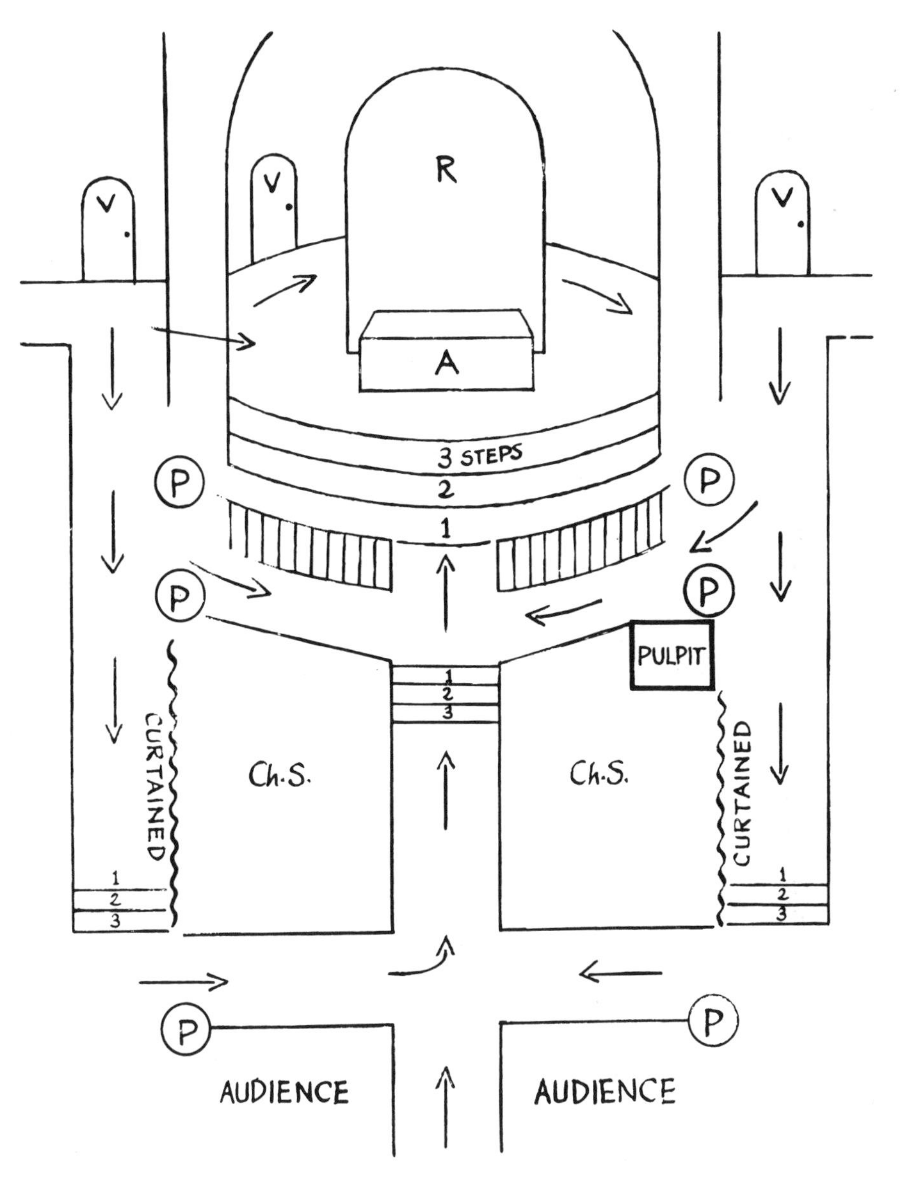

V — Vestry for changing

A — Altar covered with black material

Pulpit — Narrator sat here

P — Pillars used for lighting

Ch. S — Choirstalls

One large beam of light was operated from the balcony at the back of the church.

About three rehearsals from the end it was necessary to make over a complete afternoon to the lighting people. This is rather tedious for the actors but very necessary for the final effect. The second-from-last rehearsal became the 'dress' rehearsal, reserving the last one for polishing the timing and lighting.

At the end of it all, everyone taking part felt that it had been worthwhile and the audience seemed to appreciate the efforts of everyone concerned. It has to be remembered, though, that those who benefit the most from such a production are those who put the most into it—the team who present the pageant; hopefully, though, something came through to the audience and certainly with the lighting and high standard of costume, the production was colourful and spectacular.

Production Notes

These notes should be studied in conjunction with the full script, printed here.

All sound—music and voice—was pre-recorded. All action was therefore mimed and synchronisation and timing of action was *most* important, taking much rehearsal before it was perfected.

The 'Narrator' was in modern dress and told the story (by mime) from a dais to the right of the main action which took place in the Sanctuary of the church. Lighting and a few sound effects played their part in the effectiveness of the pageant.

The Voices referred to in the script were taped beforehand and no one was seen to speak these parts. Often the voices came through when the church was in darkness.

At the start the voice was heard in a completely darkened church. The torch bearer (dressed in a long simple robe) walked the whole length of the aisle, followed by a spotlight, until she stood in front of the altar. The music used for the torch-bearer's walk was 'Nimrod—Enigma Variations' by Elgar. The spotlight was extinguished when the Narrator spoke and a red light came on to the dais during that speech. Four young dancers, in black with a large black sheet of terylene-type material, then 'danced' their victory over the light (torch-bearer), ending by snuffing out the candle and covering the torch-bearer with the material. The music for the dance drama was 'Finlandia' by Sibelius (or part of it).

The pattern of the lights switching off at the end of each scene and on to the Narrator and so on continued throughout the pageant.

The scene of "Adam and Eve" was mimed to part of 'In the South' by Elgar. Adam and Eve were dressed in 'animal skins' with the Angel guarding the Tree of Knowledge dressed traditionally in a long robe. The action was of Adam and Eve trying to reach the tree, the Angel barring their every attempt.

In the 'Worship of Idols' scene the music was 'Belshazzar's Feast Improvisations' by William Walton. The action depicted the evil ways of Israel and Judah in worshipping of idols, drunkenness, stealing etc. On either side of the Sanctuary were idols—a golden ram and a goddess. People brought their gifts and sacrifices to the idols. A group of children ran to steal some of the fruit being offered. A drunken party took place at the bottom of the chancel steps. (Great care has to be exercised that there is not too much going on at one time to create confusion in the eye of the audience. Lighting depicted each part of the proceedings in turn, to try to avoid this pitfall.)

The 'Murder and Confusion' scene was mimed to a continuation of 'Belshazzar's Feast'. About 15-20 characters took part. Groups of twos and threes started from different points at the edge of the Sanctuary and behind the altar and ran a course from point A to point B to point C in different order. The effect was of people coming from all directions in a great state of turmoil. The lighting was blue with a continuing flashing white light and a thunder effect as well as the music.

The music chosen for the 'Hebrew Slaves taken into captivity' was the end part of Schubert's 'Unfinished Symphony'. We used as many people as possible in this scene, all dressed very similarly in brown or grey tunics and sandals. Four soldiers also took part, carrying leather whips. Slaves—in a sort of crocodile—made their way across the transept, up to the sanctuary and across the stage to behind the altar. The action was of exhausted, dejected people being harassed by the soldiers.

In 'Isaiah's' scene, a group of people on the sanctuary steps (backs to audience) looked at 'Isaiah' who mimed his message (Isaiah 60:1-5 and 18-19 (NEB)). Isaiah's voice was superimposed over horn music from 'Tristan and Isolde' by Wagner.

At this point the house lights were brought up and the audience was invited to sing 'Arise, Shine', led by a group of young singers with guitar. This gave a natural break to the history of the Old Testament and to the start of the story of the coming of Jesus, the Light of the World.

In the 'John the Baptist' scene no music was used at all. Instead the actors mimed their words, the crowd gathered around John, questioning him about his ministry and whether or not he was the promised Messiah. It finished with the crowd asking John if they could go with him to the River Jordan to be baptised. Again, because of synchronisation of voice and action, this scene needed quite a bit of rehearsal.

The Nativity was a simple tableau with Mary, Joseph, the baby and a crib. A real baby was used to add authenticity. The original candle used by the torch-bearer was placed behind the Holy Family on the altar. The music was from Handel's 'Messiah,' 'For Unto us a Child is Born.'

Rubinstein's 'Kammennoi-Ostrow' was the music chosen for the 'Shepherds in the Fields'. Around a fire were gathered four or five shepherds going about their jobs. The appearance of the Angel (from behind the altar)—spotlit and with a fan to blow her robe—caused them to react with fright. Small angels (about nine more) joined the Angel Gabriel to make a picturesque tableau. When angels departed, shepherds were seen to leave their sheep and make for the stable.

For the 'Shepherds at the Stable' Valerius' 'Prayer of Thanksgiving' was used. The Holy Family received the shepherds who worshipped the baby. This scene can be prolonged with the Shepherds making their way down the church (in a spotlight) to the stable. After kneeling to worship the shepherds returned rejoicing the way they came.

The music for 'Simeon in the Temple' was the Nunc Dimittis sung in plainsong (by the actor 'Simeon', who mimed it at the performance). The action was of Mary and Joseph with the baby. Simeon walked over to the couple and Mary handed the child to him. After the Nunc Dimittis, Simeon handed the child back and the lights faded.

In the scene 'Healing of the Blind Man' the action was based on the story of Blind Bartimaeus as told by St. Luke. The musical background to the mime was 'Introduction and Allegro for Strings' by Elgar. A group of people, including Bartimaeus, sat central on sanctuary steps. Jesus, with a following of disciples and crowd, walked across transept in front of altar rail. Hearing the accompanying crowd noise, Bartimaeus attracted Jesus' attention; Jesus went to Bartimaeus, healed him and then stepped back from the excited crowd, standing quietly for a moment before going on his way. Crowd, with Bartimaeus, giving thanks, followed Jesus at a distance.

In 'Gethsemane' the lights picked up the background vision of Jesus with three disciples whilst the Narrator was still talking (at point **** in the script). When light came off the Narrator the musical background took over—'Leylines Glassdom' by Steve Hillage Green. The disciples were seen gradually to tire and sink down to sleep. Jesus struggled with his feelings and in prayer. Lighting was bluish and at the beginning and end the sound of wind in trees could be heard. A fan blew Jesus' robe very gently to add to this effect. Finally Jesus was seen to submit and accept his Father's will.

The original dancers of Darkness and Light returned to depict the triumph of light over darkness, with the torch-bearer now triumphant, having converted the other dancers to respect the light. The final movement was of the torch-bearer (with original lighted candle on altar) standing on an elevation, arms outstretched forming a cross; other dancers stood and knelt in steps at her feet facing her. The music for this dance was part of 'In the South' by Elgar. A cross-shaped spotlight lit up the final tableau, holding its position for a short while before being raised to shine above the altar.

The dancers dispersed once the spot was off them; the torch-bearer took up the lighted candle and stood on the chancel steps, holding the torch high. Light was on the Narrator who explained the candlelight ceremony that followed. The cast lined up on either side of the chancel steps. In turn they lit their candle from the torch-bearer's candle and then moved in crocodile up the centre aisle, stopping in line with a row of the congregation. The congregation, who had candles, had theirs lit from the cast's candles until all candles were lit. During this action the voices of Readers could be heard.

Finally the dais was lit up again, the Narrator said his final piece. Then by candlelight the congregation and cast and audience sang the hymn 'Thou whose Almighty Word'. In the last verse the cast walked in procession up the aisle and off the stage.

The Pageant finished with the Vicar giving the blessing shown on the script.

A drawing of the main part of the church used in the pageant

'DARKNESS AND LIGHT'

[*Church in complete darkness*]

Voice: In the beginning of creation when God made heaven and earth, the earth was without form and void with darkness over the face of the abyss and a mighty wind that swept over the surface of the waters. God said 'Let there be light' and there was light and God saw that the light was good.

[*Light comes up on Narrator who is sitting to the right on rostrum*]

Narrator: So in the beginning we had both darkness and light.

Light was the first thing God made. It symbolised everything that was of God, whereas the darkness portrayed the absence of God.

From the beginning of the world there was a struggle to see whether the light would overcome the darkness or whether the darkness would absorb the light. To obey God was to walk in the light; to disobey God was to choose to walk in darkness. All through the history of mankind there has been a struggle between good and evil, obedience and disobedience. It is man's choice since God, in his wisdom, gave man freedom to choose which way he would go.

We now unfold the story of the struggle between darkness and light, through words, drama, music and dance.

[*Light fades on Narrator.*]

Dance Drama at altar

Narrator: [*lights up*]: Now see the first encounter that evil has with goodness in the fall of man in the Garden of Eden. Because of disobedience man is banished from the presence and knowledge of God and is cast into outer darkness.

[*Light fades on Narrator.*]

SCENE 1 'Adam and Eve' at altar

Narrator [*lights up*]: As mankind grew and multiplied, so God took pity on his people and tried to draw them back to himself. He chose a specially devout man called Abraham on whose obedience he founded the Hebrew nation. This nation was to be the means whereby he would bring his wayward creation back to himself. It was a hard task since men continually disobeyed God and rejected the laws given to them. Listen to this passage from the second book of Kings.

Voice: The Lord had sent his messengers and prophets to warn Israel and Judah: 'Abandon your evil ways and obey my commands which are contained in the Law I gave to your ancestors and which I handed on to you through my servants the prophets.' But they would not obey; they were stubborn like their ancestors who had not trusted in the Lord their God.

They refused to obey his instructions, they did not keep the covenant he had made with their ancestors and they disregarded his warnings. They worshipped worthless idols and became worthless themselves and they followed the customs of the surrounding nations disobeying the Lord's command not to imitate them.

SCENE 2 'The Worship of Idols'

Narrator [*lights up*]: We must try to remember how difficult it must have been for the Hebrews to follow the laws of God. His way of life for them was not half so attractive as the one offered by the people who lived around them and whose culture was so different; and so it was that gradually the nation ceased to listen to the prophets that God sent—Jeremiah, Isaiah, Micah, Hosea and Amos. They all had the same message—to turn from the darkness of evil and disobedience before it was too late; God would punish them if they continued to flout his law.

Voice: Ezekiel 7: from v.23

Everything is in confusion—the land is full of murders and the cities are full of violence. I will bring the most evil nations here and let them have your homes. Your strongest men will lose their confidence when I let the nations profane the places where you worship. Despair is coming. You will look for peace and never find it. One disaster will follow another and a steady stream of bad news will pour in. I will punish you for all you have done and will judge you in the same way as you have judged others. This will show you that I am the Lord.

SCENE 3 'Murder and Confusion'

Narrator [*lights up*]: And so it came to pass as God had foretold— the Hebrews were defeated in battle and taken prisoner into Babylon.

SCENE 4 'Hebrew slaves taken into captivity'

Narrator [*lights up*]: Here was darkest despair. God appeared to have abandoned his chosen people. Their cities were in ruins, their land taken over by a foreign power and their temple razed to the ground. What was there for them now? Once again just when they were crushed and helpless, God sent the light of his Word to strengthen and encourage them. His servant Isaiah gave them a message full of hope. They would return to their land and rebuild their lives for God had a special purpose for his chosen people. They would bring light to the whole world and through them all nations would be blessed.

SCENE 5 'Crowd listening to Isaiah reading his message'

(Isaiah 60: 1-5 and 18-19 (GNB))

[*House lights up for singing of 'Arise, Shine'*]

Narrator [*lights up*]: Gradually over the centuries the Hebrews returned to Jerusalem and rebuilt the Temple, restored their barren land and settled down again. But, as before, they disobeyed God and failed to listen to his Word. There were some devout people, however, who began to take notice of the prophecies that foretold the coming of a great leader—a king who would bring peace to their war-torn land and a light to their nation; they called him the Messiah. Any prophet who spoke with authority was questioned carefully—as we hear now when John the Baptist answers the people who come to him.

SCENE 6 'John the Baptist'

Narrator [*lights up*]: The scene is now set for the birth of Jesus— the light of the world—and St. John describes it like this:

Voice: Before the world was created the Word already existed; he was with God and he was the same as God. From the very beginning the Word was with God. Through him God made all things; not one thing in all creation was made without him. The Word was the source of life and this life brought light to mankind. The light shines in the darkness and the darkness has never put it out.

SCENE 7 'Nativity Scene'

Narrator: There were some shepherds in that part of the country who were spending the night in the fields, taking care of their flocks. An angel of the Lord appeared to them. They were terribly afraid but the angel said to them, 'Don't be afraid! I am here with good news for you which will bring great joy to all the people. This very day in David's town your Saviour was born—Christ the Lord! And this is what will prove it to you; you will find a baby wrapped in strips of cloth and lying in a manger.' Suddenly a great army of heaven's angels appeared with the angel singing praises to God.

SCENE 8 'Shepherds in the fields'

Narrator: When the angels went away from them back into heaven the shepherds said one to another, 'Let's go to Bethlehem and see this thing that has happened which the Lord has told us.' So they hurried off and found Mary and Joseph and saw the babe lying in the manger. When the shepherds saw the baby they told everyone they met what the angel had said about the child. Mary remembered all these things and thought deeply about them. The shepherds went back singing praises to God for all they had heard and seen; it had been just as the angel had told them.

SCENE 9 'Shepherds at the stable'

Narrator [*lights up*]: The time came for Joseph and Mary to perform the ceremony of purification as the Law of Moses commanded. So they took the child to Jerusalem to present him to the Lord, as it is written in the law of the Lord 'every first-born male is to be dedicated to the Lord'. At that time there was a man named Simeon living in Jerusalem. He was a good, devout man and was waiting for Israel to be saved. The Holy Spirit was with him and had assured him that he would not die before he had seen the Lord's promised Messiah. Led by the Spirit, Simeon went into the Temple. When the parents brought the child Jesus into the Temple, Simeon took the child in his arms and gave thanks to God.

SCENE 10 'Simeon in the Temple'

Narrator [*lights up*]: After all these things Joseph and Mary returned to their home town of Nazareth in Galilee. The child grew and became strong; he was full of wisdom and God's blessing was upon him.

Jesus was 30 when he began his ministry and immediately he challenged any areas of darkness he found. People's understanding of God was limited; they were 'in the dark' about the nature of their creator but Jesus said, 'He that has seen me has seen the Father'. Their search was over. Those who lived in despair, pain or guilt, flocked to him to be healed—each person's darkness was met and their sadness turned to joy.

SCENE 11 'Healing of Blind Man'

Narrator [*lights up*]: As Jesus' ministry continued, hostility grew towards him. The Jewish leaders and those in authority became afraid of his popularity and power over the people, but most of all they were afraid that their own hypocrisy and evil ways would be shown up against his life of purity and love—the light had to be put out!

As the time drew near for his arrest, Jesus went to pray in the garden of Gethsemane. Here we see a struggle between darkness and light within Jesus himself. Was he to obey his Father and be obedient unto death or was he to take the road of darkness and use his divine power to save himself?

SCENE 12 'Gethsemane'

[*Lights come up on tableau at **** Music starts when narrator finishes.*]

Narrator [*lights up*]: The acceptance of his Father's will signalled the Victory which we witnessed on Easter Day. Never again would the world of darkness prevail. Perfect love had been the channel through which the victory was won. Light was triumphant.

Dance drama at altar

[*Spot 'cross' finally takes lights off dancers to above altar. Dancers disperse. Torch-bearer appears with torch.*]

Narrator: We have followed the story of the conflict between darkness and light as told in the Bible; now it is time to bring it to the present age.

[*Candlelight ceremony starts.*]

As you light your candle from another and, in turn, light someone else's, listen to the advice St. John and St. Paul gave to the early Church. They used the symbols of darkness and light continually to illustrate the new life they should be living through the grace of Christ and the power of the Holy Spirit. It is just as true for us today as when they wrote it.

Readers

1. From 1st letter of St. John — 1 John 1: 5-7

Now the message that we have heard from his son and announce is this: God is light and there is no darkness at all in him. If then we say that we have fellowship with God and yet, at the same time, we live in the darkness, we are lying both in our words and our actions. But if we live in the light then we have fellowship with one another and, in the blood of Jesus, his son purifies us from every sin.

2. — 1 John 2: 9-11

Whoever says that he is in the light yet hates his brother, is in the darkness to this very hour. Whoever loves his brother, lives in the light and so there is nothing in him that will cause someone else to sin. But whoever hates his brother is in the darkness; he walks in darkness and does not know where he is going because the darkness has made him blind.

3. From Paul's letter to the Ephesians — Ch 5: 8-9

You yourselves used to be in the darkness, but since you have become the Lord's people you are in the light. So you must live like people who belong to the light, for it is the light that brings a rich harvest of every kind of goodness, righteousness and truth.

4. — Ch 5: 10-11

Try to learn what pleases the Lord; have nothing to do with the worthless things that people do, things that belong to the darkness. Instead bring them out to the light.

5. — Ch 5: 13-14

And when all things are brought out to the light then their true nature is clearly revealed; for anything that is clearly revealed becomes light.

6. From Paul's letter to the Philippians — Ch 2: 14-15

Do everything without complaining or arguing so that you may be innocent and pure as God's perfect children who live in a world of corrupt and sinful people. You must shine among them as stars lighting up the sky.

7. From Paul's letter to the Colossians Ch 3: 12-

You are the people of God; he loved you and chose you for his own. So then, you must clothe yourselves with compassion, kindness, humility, gentleness and patience.

8. 13

Be tolerant with one another and forgive one another whenever any of you has a complaint against someone else. You must forgive one another just as the Lord has forgiven you.

9. 14-15

And to all these qualities add love, which binds all things together in perfect unity. The peace that Christ gives is to guide you in the decisions you make; for it is to this peace that God has called you together in the one body.

Narrator: And be thankful. Christ's message in all its richness must live in your hearts. Teach and instruct each other with all wisdom; sing psalms, hymns and sacred songs; sing to God with thanksgiving in your hearts. Everything you do or say, then, should be done in the name of the Lord Jesus, as you give thanks through him to God the Father.

Vicar [*live*]: And may the Lord himself, who is our source of peace and light, give you his peace and light at all times and in every way. The Lord be with you all.

Hymn: 'Thou whose Almighty Word'

BLESSING

GOOD FRIDAY IS TODAY

'A kind of play for young people'
by Gordon Turvey

Production Notes
The play was first performed on Good Friday in Christ Church, Radlett. The action took place in the Choir and on a platform erected in front of it. Duration 30-35 minutes. Scene 3 is optional if the performance is on Good Friday, as it may be thought more suitable for Easter Sunday only.

The cast of 20 in Scene 1 doubled for other scenes. Their ages ranged from 11 to 17 (the commentator). A choir, unrobed, helped the singing. The songs are to be found in *Faith, Folk and Festivity* and *Faith, Folk and Clarity,* published by Galliard, the hymns in *Ancient and Modern Revised* (AMR).

To emphasize the relevance for today, everyday clothes were worn, even by the procession into Jerusalem. The two Pharisees whom Judas accosts should wear a simple cloak or scarf suitable for members of the Sanhedrin, but at their second entrance, as Sheikhs, they wear modern dress with an Arab headdress. In Scene 2, the Sanhedrin wear very simple over-garments of a variety of colours, with Caiaphas more gaudily dressed and with a headdress if desired. Peter and the young man and girl are in modern dress and so are those in Scene 3. *(It would be a help to start with an organ voluntary in which the melody of 'Jerusalem' was recognisable.)*

NB. Black man must be genuine: make-up will not do. If not available, cut his first speech, and Bertie takes this part later.

[*A Commentator enters, comes down the centre and up into the pulpit.*]

Commentator: At this time of Holy Week and Good Friday the countryside of England does indeed become a green and pleasant land with the prospect of spring. But in this church this afternoon we must use our imagination to compare it with the Green Hill of Calvary, far away, outside the walls of Jerusalem. Perhaps we may wonder, as Blake did, whether those feet of Jesus in ancient times, *did* walk upon England's mountains green.

What if he came to [*name own town*] and walked down our streets? There would be much to cause him to wonder; much to cause us shame as we think of the complications of our lives—the strife and selfishness—the greed of our society—the hardship caused by unemployment. Think of the frustration of young people today who feel themselves unwanted because no one will employ them.

Man: [*rising from a seat in the church and coming to the centre*] : You talk about unemployment, mate. Why 'ave we got unemployment? I'll tell you. All them wogs, that's why. Pinchin' our jobs.

Commentator: Just a minute—

Man: Oh no? You stop immigration an' send 'em back to their own country an' we won't 'ave no unemployment. England's green and pleasant land for the National Front. Yeah! A land of hope and glory! You keep it like that, mate.

Black Man [*enters*] : You're not being fair to black people, my friend. I'm black, but I was born here. My father's a doctor at the hospital. I'm as British as you are, but *I* can't get a job; and that's because of my colour. It's unfair and wrong to discriminate against coloured people.

Second Man [*enters*]: It's the likes of him keep our wages down. He'd take a job at any price, but I've got my family to keep. Four kids and a mortgage to pay. How am I to get enough to keep them living decent? And prices going up all the time. How am I to do that? Nick it? Steal it?

[*Lady and Gentleman have come down the centre to join the group and a Third Man and a Woman enter*] .

Lady: Oh no! You mustn't do that! I'm sure we could help you. Perhaps we could run a coffee morning for you and your friends. What do you think about that, Bertie?

Bertie: I don't really know. I'm in the City all day. It doesn't really affect me.

Third Man: Oh no! I don't suppose it does. You've got all the money you need. Two cars and a yacht, I expect. On expense account, I'll bet. But that doesn't help me.

Bertie: Oh, I say!

Woman: You've got to look after yourself these days. No one else will do it, in spite of what *she* says. Use your brains, Charlie. I make quite a nice bit from the things I bring out of the factory in my car boot. I can sell 'em and no questions asked! Anyway it's safer than pushing drugs, I can tell you.

First Man: Well, I think it's a disgrace, the rackets some of you people get up to. No wonder the country's going down hill. The whole thing wants cleaning up—the political system, the vandalism, the lot. The whole thing wants cleaning up.

Black Man: And what would you put in its place when you had cleaned it up?

Third Man: Well, Mr. Smart Alec, I'll tell you. A revolution, that's what. A ruddy revolution.

Second Man: I won't stand for that nonsense. I've got too much to lose. I've got four kids to look after.

First Man: [*with sarcasm*] : And your mortgage to pay!

Second Man: I don't want any of your Communism here.

Lady: Oh no! We mustn't have the Communists here. They take all one's money away, don't they, Bertie?

Black Man [*to Second Man*] : Then what sort of revolution do *you* want?

Woman: I don't want no revolution. I'm all right my way.

Third Man: Cowards! That's what you all are. Daren't face it! Cowards! You don't realise what the working class stands to gain when all the rich people have been done away with. Cowards!

First Man: It can only be done if we join together and fight for the National Front.

Second Man: It's you and your lot who are ruining the country.

Woman: And getting into all the Unions. We've got our own way of doing things—nice an' comfy—till some of your lot start agitating.

[*An argument develops with shouts of 'Up the reds', 'Up the fascists'. A procession has entered from some other part of the church, singing the hymn 'All glory, laud and honour' to guitar accompaniment with tambourines, etc., and girls dancing. Palms could be carried by a few. There are occasional shouts of 'Hosanna to the Son of David'.*]

Second Man: What's the meaning of all this?

[*The group stares in amazement. The procession mingles with the group, singing stops, and when it is quiet enough to hear, the Man says to a disciple*] :

First Man: What's all this about?

First Disciple: We've come up to Jerusalem with Jesus of Nazareth.

First Man: Have you come to join the revolution?

First Disciple: Yes, of course.

Second Disciple: Yes! We ARE the revolution!

[*More cheers from disciples, who start singing 'All glory . . . ' again (chorus only). They mingle with the group and extol the revolution, each taking a phrase in turn such as:*]

We're starting the New Age.

What John the Baptist talked about.

We have come to the Kingdom of God.

He overturned the market stalls in the Temple.

He called the Pharisees whitewashed sepulchres!

He told us to love our enemies.

He will be the Saviour of Israel.

Jesus will make everything new.

He heals the sick and crippled.

Jesus casts out the Devil.

Jesus' revolution will make us all children of God.

Guitarist [*going up to altar rail*]: Come on! Shout Hosanna! [*He strikes a chord, and everyone, except Communist and Fascist, gathers round, grouped on choir stalls if necessary, and sings 'When they shouted Hosanna'* (New Life, Galliard/Stainer & Bell). *Choir joins in. Verses 1, 2 and 5 may suffice. Communist and Fascist unobtrusively in argument at one side until the singing ends and the whole crowd disperses*].

First Man [*to Judas, one of the disciples*]: Here a minute.

Judas [*coming down centre*]: What is it?

First Man: Are you the leader of these people?

Judas: No, Jesus is our leader. I'm Judas Iscariot. I'm just one of his disciples, but Jesus is our leader. He teaches us about the coming of the Kingdom of God, but I'm afraid he's very slow in bringing about the changes necessary for the New Age.

Third Man: A new age?

Judas: Do you know, the other day someone asked him about paying taxes to Caesar. It was just the question to unite the people against the Romans. He could have said, "No, don't pay", and the crowd would have followed him anywhere. But what did he say? "Give to Caesar what belong to Caesar". Such a great opportunity missed. He's too gentle.

Third Man: You need to be brutal in a revolution, comrade. Make him take a lead. Force him to act.

Judas: Yes, but how? How can you do that with someone who has thought it all out? He knows what God's will is for him.

Third Man: Well, put him on the spot. Why not get him arrested? Fear always makes a man act and act quickly.

First Man [*laughing*] : That's a bright idea, I will say! Get him arrested! Well, good luck. [*All except Judas leave*] .

Judas [*in deep thought*] : Get him arrested. I wonder if that would work. Yes, arrested by the Jews! Then he'd have to do something. And the crowds would throng round to support him. [*With growing enthusiasm*] . The Hosts of Israel—ready for anything—for sabotage—for massacre! The liberation army! We'd sweep the Romans into the sea.

[*Hurries up centre to follow the crowd, but two Pharisees, slowly walking down and talking, pass him. He stops in his tracks, turns, and impulsively calls after them as they have almost gone off*] .

Judas: Hi! Excuse me!

First Pharisee: Yes, my friend?

Judas: May I speak to you for a moment? [*They turn and join Judas in centre.*] . You are members of the Sanhedrin, are you not?

First Pharisee; Yes. I am Shadrach. This is Councillor Issachar. What can we do for you?

Judas: I am a disciple of Jesus of Nazareth. I think you might like to know more about him and what his plans are.

Second Pharisee: Yes, indeed we should.

Judas: I realise that some of the things he says are critical of the rulers of our nation . . . perhaps unwisely. Would you like to have him in your power—just for a short time? Perhaps he could be arrested. It might teach him a lesson.

First Pharisee: Yes, that's an interesting idea. Let us talk a little more about it.

[*The three move up together and stand talking at the altar rail. The Choir sings 'Lord of the Dance'. During the last verse, one of the Pharisees hands Judas the bag of silver. Exeunt*] .

Commentator [*from pulpit*] : No! It won't work! Many have tried to win by force. Hitler . . . Amin . . . but in the long run governing by fear won't work. We can't bring in the Kingdom of God by terrorism and bombs. His rule is a rule of love where men are reconciled to one another, and at peace with God. Do the nations of the world believe this? They know what Judas did. Do our ministers and officials know this? Or do we still betray our Lord today?

[*A Government Official (played by 'Judas'), in a smart suit and with despatch case, enters, goes up centre, and on his way passes two sheikhs (played by 'Shadrach' and 'Issachar') slowly walking up and down and talking. The Official stops in his tracks, turns, and impulsively calls after them as they have almost gone off, the movements being exactly the same as for Judas and the Pharisees.*]

Official: Hi! Excuse me.

First Sheikh [*slight Arab accent*]: Yes, my friend?

Official: May I speak to you for a moment? [*They turn and join the Official in the centre.*]. You are officials of the oil-producing countries, are you not?

First Sheikh: Yes. I am Abdul Ahmed. This is Sheikh Ali Moustapha. What can we do for you?

Official: I represent a very large armament production Group in the western world. [*Hand-shaking all round*]. May I put a suggestion to you two gentlemen? We know that the present situation in Arab countries is difficult, and in the interests of both of us we ought to come to some agreement with you; you to supply our western countries with oil, and we to sell you armaments. We now have some really powerful nuclear weapons.

Second Sheikh: Yes. That would put us in a very strong position in the Middle East.

Official: I am sure that with the weapons we can supply the Arab countries could be in control in the Middle East. But you must, in return, guarantee our oil supply.

First Sheikh: I understand.

Official: We have invested a great deal of capital in nuclear arms, and now, at all costs, we must build up our export trade in them. Would you like to consider a trade treaty between us?

First Sheikh: Yes. It's an interesting idea. Let us talk a little more about it.

[*The three move up together and stand talking at the altar rail, in the position as Judas did.*

The Choir sing 'Good Friday' to guitar. Omit verse 4. At verse 5 the bargain has been concluded, Sheikhs and Official shake hands and exeunt. The Congregation sings 'My song is love unknown' AMR 102, omitting verses 4 and 6].

SCENE 2

[*An imposing chair has been set on a small central rostrum for Caiaphas. The Sanhedrin enters, informally, chatting, and sits. Steward enters, followed by Caiaphas, who is ushered to his 'throne'. Sanhedrin stands while he enters, then sits. Traders sit in front of the stage and mainly out of sight.*]

Steward: [*Thumping his staff*]: Silence in Court! [*Coming forward to the congregation, who are treated as part of the Sanhedrin*]: Please take your seats for the continuation of the trial of Jesus of Nazareth before the High Priest Caiaphas. Silence in Court!

Caiaphas [*standing*]: We will now continue with the evidence we heard at our last session. I call on Shadrach. [*sits*].

Shadrach [*each member stands to speak*]: My Lord Caiaphas and Councillors, at our previous meeting we heard about the violence which took place the other day in the Temple. Jesus attacked traders, overturned their stalls, and called honest men thieves.

Traders [*From below*]: He did. Yes, he did. Called us thieves!

Shadrach: He scattered their produce, and many . . .

Traders: A shame. It was a shame. Such waste of good fruit!

Shadrach: Many of them are poor farmers and can't afford such losses.

Traders [*getting worked up*]: Hear, hear! We can't afford it. [*Steward gets up and makes to restore order*]. That's true. Such a waste.

Shadrach: And he also interrupted the legitimate business of the Temple money-lenders.

Now this is a serious matter, but it is not an offence sufficiently serious to condemn Jesus to be handed over to . . .

Traders [*vociferous*]: Nonsense. It's very serious. We lost a lot of money. My stall was smashed up. *That's* serious. He upset all my oranges. I can't afford to lose money. He let all my pigeons go and broke up my baskets. He deserves to be punished. Interfering with our rightful trade. It's a shame.

Steward [*stalking round with his staff during this outburst*]: Silence in Court. Order please! Silence!

Shadrach: I repeat, we need evidence of a much more serious offence to enable this Sanhedrin to condemn Jesus and be rid of him, and that offence is blasphemy. He made himself out to be Son of God, and actually claimed that he forgave a man's sins, which only God can do.

Issachar: And there is something else. He has criticised our Holy Laws and made us Pharisees look ridiculous. This is worse than blasphemy.

Third Councillor: He said that a sinner going to the Temple to ask God for mercy was more in the right than we who pay a tenth of all our possessions and fast twice a week!

Issachar: This cavalier way of criticising and ridiculing our holy profession affects our livelihood and the whole security of the State of Israel. [*With emphasis*]: If we allow the Law of Moses—the laws of our nation—to be undermined, there will be anarchy! We need to alert our police to repress any free-thinking of this sort. There can be no freedom allowed to people who want to re-write our laws and to proclaim a new Commandment, as Jesus does. *We* are appointed to be God's interpreters and to protect our way of life. Death is too good for any traitors of this sort.

Nicodemus: I think, my Lord, that in these times of change we should be prepared to move with the times. We must seek the guidance of Almighty God in this matter and not be seen to be fighting against his will.

Third Councillor: Is Nicodemus also one of his disciples? [*Shouts and jeers from other Council members*].

Caiaphas: One at a time, please.

Fourth Councillor: One other thing. Councillor Issachar mentioned our livelihood. Jesus has more than hinted that we make a dishonest living out of our professional fees and quite legitimate expenses.

Other Councillors: Hear, hear!

Fifth Councillor: He called us whitewashed sepulchres!

Fourth Councillor: This lowers our standard of living, at a time of inflation, it is not only our standards which are affected but those of the whole country. We must not be encouraged to 'give away our cloaks', as Jesus once said. It is our duty to see that no one is worse off. Our standards of living must not be allowed to fall.

Sixth Councillor: My Lord, I am a traditionalist. What was right for my fathers is good enough for me, and I do not want to see any changes made—moving with the times indeed! [*pointing at Nicodemus*]: There must be no changes in our holy faith nor in the ritual worship in the Temple. There must be no rebellion against our established ways.

Caiaphas: Do you fear there might be a rebellion, Senator?

Sixth Councillor: Well, yes, my Lord, I do. This man Jesus associates with the most degraded people—women and so on—and he has a very strong following among the poor. They flock to hear him and to be healed, including outcasts and lepers! These are just the sort of people to cause a rebellion under a popular leader.

Shadrach: My Lord Caiaphas, may I say again that while some of the accusations made against Jesus are extremely serious, the sin we cannot tolerate is blasphemy. Jesus the Nazarene claimed he was sent by God and that he was the promised Messiah.

Caiaphas [*standing*]: Thank you, gentlemen. [*Comes down centre. The Steward stands too*]. It is my opinion that we have heard enough evidence to enable us to come to a verdict. There are three important issues I ask you to consider. [*Referring to his notes*]: First, it is clear that Jesus is intent on degrading our holy calling as Pharisees. He is determined to destroy our authority as teachers of people and custodians of the Holy Laws given us by God.

It follows that the people are being encouraged to think for themselves. This is dangerous; for you will see that behind such teaching is the idea that all men are equal before God—the poor as well as the rich, the sinners as well as those who keep the Law. Seditious ideas like that may very well lead to a breach of the peace, and we do NOT want the Roman authorities provoked to violence.

Councillors: Hear, hear!

Caiaphas: Secondly, Jesus has the presumption to give the people what he calls a New Commandment, to love one another. I do *not* want to see brotherly love with the enemies of Israel [*hear, hear!*] He teaches people to put this 'law' into practice and asks them to be tolerant and forgiving to evil-doers. He expects his disciples to care for the poor and the sick—that is *our* duty. He actually sends these disciples, who after all are only peasants and fishermen, to try to heal the sick. That's what he calls his New Commandment. And thirdly . . .

Fifth Councillor [*interrupting*] : He called us whitewashed sepulchres.

Caiaphas [*impatiently*] : Yes, yes. Thirdly, there is the charge of blasphemy, as Senator Shadrach has reminded us. When we asked Jesus if he was the Christ, the Son of God, he said he was. The idea of our God [*with emotional emphasis*] Jehovah the Almighty, whose throne is in Heaven, coming to live among men upon earth, among the squalor and sin of ordinary peasants, is abhorrent.

What further testimony do we need? We have heard this blasphemy ourselves from his own lips.

Councillors: Guilty! Guilty! Blasphemy is worthy of death. [*General clamour which Traders applaud*] .

Caiaphas: Thank you, Councillors. [*Coming to the front to the congregation*] : You have heard the evidence, ladies and gentlemen. Have you anything you wish to add? Then the trial is concluded. [*He tears up his notes and scatters them*] .

[*Exeunt Traders and Sanhedrin noisily.*
Remove Caiaphas' chair.
Peter, who has been sitting unobtrusively in front throughout, comes to warm his hands at a brazier—imagined—in the centre. A young man enters followed by a girl] .

Young Man: Hello, Peter! Fancy meeting you here! [*to the girl*] : I say, here's Peter the Fisherman.

Young Girl: What are you doing here, Peter? Been listening to the trial?

Peter: Oh no. Nothing. Just warming my hands.

Young Man: But you're a member of [*name own church*] aren't you? I thought you'd be interested in the fate of Jesus.

Peter: Oh no! I don't really know him.

Young Girl: But I thought you were a follower of his.

Young Man: Surely you were with him at his last supper.

Peter: No, damn you! I tell you I don't even know the man.

Young Man: There's no need to get shirty. It doesn't matter.

Young Girl: I thought you could have told us something about him. But it doesn't really matter.
[*Exeunt*]

Peter: O my God! What have I said? [*turning to the altar*] : I have disowned you, Master. [*at the altar rail*] : O God. [*he falls across the altar, sobbing*] : O Master. O Jesus.

[*Soprano soloist very quietly begins to sing 'Were you there when they crucified my Lord?' Choir joins in at the second verse. Peter reaches to a wooden cross placed on the altar for Good Friday. Last verse sung with triumph.*]

SCENE 3 (Optional)

[*The Commentator enters and goes to the centre. Two excited girls enter, as in the Resurrection scene from 'Christ is Alive', page 31*].

Commentator: Hello girls. You seem very excited on this lovely morning. What's it all about?

First Girl: Oh yes! We've got some wonderful news.

Second Girl: We've just been to the tomb. It's a miracle.

Commentator: What's happened?

First Girl: Mary and I went to the cave this morning and—you know the huge stone that twenty of us had rolled over the entrance? Well, it was moved back.

Second Girl: Yes, and standing there was an angel who told us unbelievable news—that Jesus was alive again!

Commentator: That Jesus was alive again?

First Girl: Yes. So Mary ran to tell the men who were coming to the cave, and she ran into Jesus himself, walking through the garden.

Second Girl: You know he always said this—that he would rise again after his death. And it's true!

First Girl: Oh, it's fantastic. Well, we must dash off and tell the others in the city.

[*Exeunt excitedly. Exit Commentator. Choir sings 'The Angel rolled the stone away'* (Faith, Folk and Clarity, Galliard/Stainer & Bell)]

CONCLUSION

Commentator [*coming centre*] : Let us pray.

O Lord Jesus, on this Good Friday we remember your humiliation and torture, and your death for the sake of the world. May we never be guilty of denying you, nor of betraying you; but be witnesses to your love and risen power to cleanse and redeem the world of its evil.

You call us to be messengers of the Good News of your Resurrection; help us to answer your call with joy and in your name. *Amen.*

Let us say together the Lord's Prayer. Our Father . . .

Hymn: 'Just as I am' (AMR 349)

[*Sung by Choir and congregation, after which the Commentator may say the Grace or a dismissal*]

JAMES AND THE CHRYSALIS

A story for infants by Sarah Parkes

James saw 'IT' by the drainpipe over the back door. He climbed on to an old wooden stool to look more closely—it was brown and dirty, wrinkled like a leaf, and hanging in a spidery thread.

'Don't touch it!' his big brother called out quickly.

'It's ugly,' James said. 'I'm going to knock it down.'

'Lots of things are ugly,' said Mark, 'but we mustn't hurt them.'

'This thing isn't alive,' James said.

'Yes it is—it's called a chrysalis. Do you know what a chrysalis is, James? It's what happens when a caterpillar falls asleep. He spins himself into a funny dry-brown package and falls asleep . . .'

'A chrysalis—' James liked the word. 'A chrysalis.'

'And all the time that he's asleep,' Mark said, 'he's changing.'

'From an ugly old caterpillar?' asked James.

'Ugly or pretty, every caterpillar makes himself into a chrysalis,' Mark told him. 'And when he is asleep he changes into something really beautiful—the most beautiful thing that you can think of.'

'What's that?' James asked, looking with interest at the brown leaf-like chrysalis that hung, in its dusty thread, over his back door. 'The caterpillar-chrysalis turns into a butterfly,' his brother told him. 'One day in spring when the sun is warm, he'll wake and stretch—s-t-r-e-t-c-h—out his new wings and fly away.'

'Does he know that he's got wings?' James whispered. 'Does he know that one day he'll be a butterfly? Or does he think he's just a silly old caterpillar asleep in a dry dusty chrysalis?'

'I don't know,' his brother said.

'Who changes him?'

'God, I suppose.'

'Why?'

'Oh, James,' said Mark. 'I don't know everything. Come on, it's time to go indoors for tea.'

James thought about the chrysalis. 'Can I put it in a jam jar? he asked his brother. 'If the sun shines one day when I'm not here I shan't see the butterfly come out and s-t-r-e-t-c-h his wings.'

'He'd hate to wake and stretch and flutter, and find himself shut inside a glass jar.'

James thought about that too, and he agreed.

He waited.

Often he forgot about the caterpillar-chrysalis as he ran in and out of the back door.

But often he remembered.

One sunny day he looked up and it had gone: only dry dust was there. But in the back-yard there was a butterfly, with pretty shimmering wings dancing in the sunshine.

He called to Mark.

'Not one butterfly,' Mark said. 'I can see two!'

'Three!' James shouted. 'Which one is ours, I wonder? Aren't we lucky that they're here in our back-yard!'

THE SMASHING CLAY DOG

A story for juniors, with a theme of reconciliation, by Peter Glanville

There was a cacophony of voices, clattering desk lids, pounding fists, clinking water jars and the occasional crash as something slipped through wet fingers and smashed on the floor in a thousand fragments—Billy's class were having their art lesson. Charlie, Richard, Simon, Paul and Billy had managed to sit together on a desk set for clay work, and already clay was everywhere. All five of them had clay up to their elbows of course, but somehow Richard had managed to cover his nose as well, probably when scratching it, and Paul's hair, usually blond, was now a muddy brown.

Billy had contented himself with getting the front of his shirt, where it touched the desk, thickly coated in runny clay like lumpy gravy. 'My mum'll kill me,' he thought. But despite the mess, or perhaps because of it, they had all managed to make something to be proud of. Richard had built a tank and had even painstakingly marked in the tracks. Billy had constructed a terrifying monster with huge bulging eyes and a drooling mouth. 'I'm going to call it Sally, after my sister,' he said with a grin. Simon and Paul had worked together to make a model house, with all the details, bricks, window frames, a door-knocker, and when you lifted off the roof you could see they had even put furniture inside.

But undoubtedly the best of all was Charlie's model of a dog. Lovingly and in concentrated silence he had moulded the nose, tail, legs, stuck on the ears, changed this, added that until the dog lay with its nose on crossed paws, eyes closed, so life-like that you felt that if you breathed it would open its eyes and wag its tail. 'That's really smashing, Charlie. You're bound to get a gold star for it,' said Billy. 'When it's painted and varnished, it'll be good enough to sell,' added Richard.

'Oh, I wouldn't sell it,' said Charlie, his eyes alight with pride.

'What's his name?' asked Paul.

Charlie didn't need to think about this. He'd always wanted a dog, and had planned in his imagination what his dog would be called, what tricks he would teach it, and even which collar at the local pet shop would look the smartest. Unfortunately both his mum and dad were out to work all day, so it wasn't fair to have a dog yet—but one day! 'His name is Raggamuffin,' he said with quiet conviction.

They all agreed that this was a fine name, and after a few minutes' further admiration, everyone got back to their own work. Charlie carefully wrote a note saying 'Please don't touch', folded it so that it stood up, and put Raggamuffin over in the art corner to dry.

Bit by bit everybody finished their work, and after tidying their area and washing off the worst of the paint or clay, they sat down to do some reading. Billy was late finishing. The ears of his monster had the annoying habit of dropping off, and it had taken ages to put a little collar of clay around each ear and smooth it out, but now each ear proudly and firmly stuck out in a most fearsome fashion. Billy took his model to the art corner and put it down next to Charlie's.

Again he was captivated by the dog. It was so real that you wanted to touch it and pat its head. Tentatively, Billy reached out his finger and smoothed the dog's back. Just then, Paul, who had been leaning too far back in his chair as usual, fell over backwards with a bang and an embarrassed giggle, which made everyone jump. Billy jumped. His finger jerked uncontrollably, knocking the clay dog off of the bench on to the floor.

Billy's heart was in his mouth. Had anyone seen? No, they were too busy grinning at Paul, whilst the teacher said, 'If you can't sit on the chair properly, that's what will happen. Chairs have four legs; kindly use them all, Paul.' Quickly Billy picked Raggamuffin up off the floor, put him back next to Charlie's little sign 'Please don't touch', and looked to see if there was any damage. The model was all bent out of shape.

'Oh, why couldn't I have left it alone?' whispered Billy miserably. In desperation he tried to straighten the dog out, but his trembling fingers only succeeded in making things worse. In the end he walked away and sat down in his place. He took out his book, and tried to forget what he'd done. Perhaps it wasn't as bad as he thought. Charlie mightn't notice after all. But as he turned the pages, he knew he was lying to himself. Charlie would be heart-broken.

Just then the bell went, and they went out to play. Billy rushed out first, because he wanted to be as far away from the model as possible, but as he ran on to the playground he couldn't help noticing through the window that Charlie was going to have one last look at his dog before coming out to play. Tensely Billy watched as Charlie walked towards the bench, saw his change of expression from proud happiness to disbelieving anger and hurt. It was like watching the television with the sound turned down, but Billy knew the things that Charlie was saying. He couldn't bear to watch any longer, and rushed off to join in a game of football.

But there was no escape. He couldn't forget what he'd done, and the way Charlie had looked. He wasn't afraid of being found out, for he was sure that no-one had noticed him in the corner, but it would be really horrible if Charlie suspected someone else, or even thought that someone had deliberately ruined his dog from jealousy, or just to hurt him. Billy imagined how in a few minutes Charlie would come and tell him about what had happened, and how he would have to lie and pretend to be shocked. Charlie would pour all his misery out, and Billy would have to listen in sympathy, all the time knowing that it was all his fault.

No. It was no good. Like an elastic band stretched too tight Billy's mind snapped to a decision. He must go and tell Charlie the truth. If he didn't their friendship would never be the same again, for the lie he'd told would haunt him and make him uncomfortable. Maybe Charlie would stop being friends now, but that was a chance he would just have to take. He walked back to the classroom, and met Charlie coming out through the door. Charlie's eyes were red, and as he started to speak his voice shook, 'Someone's gone and . . .'.

'I know, Charlie, I'm very sorry, but I did it accidentally.' Billy explained quickly what had happened, watching his friend's face anxiously. Charlie listened, and when Billy had finished, he simply walked away without saying a word, his face set and white.

Billy felt like crying, but somehow he also felt relieved. Charlie was upset, but at least he'd done the right thing, he was sure of it. He spent a miserable playtime, mooning about on his own, feeling that everyone would hate him. The bell went, and he trudged back to the classroom with his hands in his pockets. Just then he felt a light touch on his shoulder. He turned, and there was Charlie. They looked at each other in silence, and then Charlie reached out, and shook Billy's hand.

'It's all right,' he said quietly, and smiled. Billy broke into a warm, relieved grin and shook hands silently. Later the other children noticed Charlie's damaged model, and were very upset about it, but Charlie just said, 'I'm afraid I accidentally dropped it—never mind.'

THE TREE

A story with implications for Passiontide, told by Sarah Parkes

Even now wolves prowl the forests of Canada. In the very cold winters they come down close to the towns for food; children hurry home on winter's evenings.

A long time ago, when my grandfather was a boy, he stayed late in the school yard skating with his friends. The school yard had been flooded and then frozen and the boys were practising keenly for the ice-hockey matches. The sun had already set, red in the cold sky, when my grandfather took off his skates and started home through the forest. At first the boy walked confidently along the path shining his torch. All sorts of horrid stories came into his head about wolves, and were-wolves too; and of trees that caught and held you in their branches. Or it might snow again and hide the path. He shook his head to get rid of the thoughts and swung his skates and shone his torch.

A tree loomed up before him. Ugly and misshapen it seemed in the black darkness. Its branches were like hands that reached out to hold him. He turned and ran off through the soft snow.

Almost at once he knew that he was lost. He knew that lost travellers often wandered hopelessly in circles instead of going straight forward to warmth and safety. He stood still and listened: no sound except the soft plop of snow as it melted from the branches. At least the temperature was not below freezing tonight!

He listened again.

A sound, far away!

It might be a train whistling as it rushed through the darkness towards the prairies.

Or it might be—wolves baying, coming closer, closing in on him. He imagined them, red-eyed, long-tongued, soft-footed.

He must climb a tree till morning. He dropped his skates. As he stood listening his torch went out. He shook it and pressed it but it would not light again. Now he was truly alone.

The trees pressed about him. He tripped over the roots of one and as he scrambled up he thought that it would be easy to climb because of its many odd-shaped branches.

He climbed gratefully—its rough, warm bark seemed to welcome him into its safety.

All night he clung there, cold but safe from wolves, if wolves there were.

In the morning he climbed down, stiff and sore and anxious at the thought of his parents' anxiety.

No fresh snow had fallen and at once he recognised the path he had been on the night before. There were his footprints where he had panicked and run off through the soft snow!

And the tree that had sheltered him all night, keeping him safe through the night? That tree was the ugly, dark shape that he had feared, that he had run away from, crying to himself: 'No! No! No!'

The tree that he had feared was the tree that had saved him.

A SERVICE FOR GOOD FRIDAY

This service for parents and children was written and conducted by Diane F. Priest

The service is a simplified form of meditation on the Stations of the Cross. Five poster-sized pictures were made beforehand by the leader, as there was not time for the children to make these themselves—if this could be arranged, perhaps in Sunday school time, it would be preferable. A strong child held these up in succession while the leader commented on them. A different child read each passage and led each prayer, the congregation joining in from duplicated copies. The whole service lasted a little under an hour.

The leader welcomes the children and explains that today we are going to hear the story of the sufferings of Jesus; we shall look at some pictures, sing some songs, and pray some prayers, to try and feel what it was like for him, and live through his sufferings with him as far as we can. The first song will tell the whole story; we'll then look at its separate parts.

Song: 'Gentle Christ, Wise and Good' (*New Orbit,* published by Galliard/Stainer and Bell)

Picture: *Jesus praying in Gethsemane, with the disciples asleep, away from him.* Leader holds or fastens this up. The leader can speak of how lonely Jesus felt, when all his friends had abandoned him. Do you ever feel lonely and abandoned? Have you ever felt afraid of a very hard or scary thing (like a visit to the dentist?) that you had to do? Jesus is afraid, but he accepts what he must do because he trusts his Father.

Reading: Mark 14.32-41

Prayer: Jesus, in the darkness of the garden
You faced your fear.
Your friends left you alone.
They were asleep when you needed them.
But you did not run away from what you had to do:
You said yes to the day ahead,
You said you would go through with it.
You chose suffering and death
For love of your friends who had left you
For love of all men everywhere.
Thank you for your courage, Lord Jesus.
Help us to know that you are with us
When things are difficult,

When we are afraid in the night,
When we are worried about what will happen.
Help us to be brave like you,
To say yes to God's plan for our lives.

Help us to be good friends,
To seek out the people who need to be loved,
To help the sad and lonely,
To listen to those who need to tell us their troubles,
And show everyone that you love them by caring for them. Amen.

Song: 'Kum ba yah' *(New Orbit)*

Picture: *Jesus being whipped.* Leader describes whip, how painful it was. Why do we inflict pain on each other? Do we have an impulse to 'lash out'? All over the world there is war, aggression, and suffering of the innocent. Yet Jesus let us hurt him and did not strike back.

Reading: Mark 15.1-15

Prayer: Lord Jesus, we think of you, cruelly whipped
Although you had done nothing wrong.
You did not deserve such a punishment:
You were innocent.

We pray for the innocent people who suffer in the world today:
The men, women and children hurt by other people's actions;
Victims of war in Asia, Africa and Ireland;
Children dying of starvation caused by others' greed.
You have felt their pain and sorrow in your own wounds.
Forgive us for our anger and hate.
Forgive us for the pleasure we sometimes have in hurting others.
Help us to control
Our wish to hit out and fight back.
Help us to love and forgive our enemies as you did. Amen.

Picture: *Jesus crowned with thorns.* Leader explains that the soldiers did this to humiliate Jesus, to make him look foolish. 'You say you're a King—here's your crown!' Do we sometimes like to bully the weak, or mock those we do not understand?

Reading: Matthew 27.27-31

Prayer: Lord Jesus,
You let the soldiers bully you.
They dressed you up,
Hit you and spat at you.
They pressed sharp thorns onto your head.
You did not cry or speak.

We are sorry that it is so easy for us
To laugh at people we do not understand.

We are sorry that sometimes we want to bully
People who are weaker than ourselves.
Forgive us, Lord Jesus,
For wanting to be better, cleverer or stronger than others.

We pray for people who are bullied or tormented
Because they are different in some way,
Because their skin is a different colour,
Because they do not believe exactly the same things as everybody else.
Help us to understand and love
People who are different from us. Amen.

Song: 'Hallelujah, My Father' (*Hymns Old and New,* published by Kevin Mayhew)

Picture: *Jesus, carrying the cross, falls under its weight, and is helped by Simon of Cyrene* (Luke 23.26, perhaps too short for a separate reading). Leader can speak of bearing one another's burdens. Let us pray for all the people everywhere who are sharing in the caring for the pain of the world.

Prayer: Lord Jesus, we think of your weariness
As you stumbled under the heavy weight of the Cross,
As you tried to carry it through the narrow streets.
We think of your bruised knees and your aching back.
We are glad that Simon was there to help you.

We pray for all those
Who find life almost too hard to bear;
Poor farmers in Asia who struggle to feed their families;
Children in South America who work to help their brothers and sisters;
And everyone who knows no rest from hardship and misery.

Help us to hear their cries for help,
Help us to share their burdens in any way we can,
Because in helping to relieve the sufferings of the weak and poor,
We are following your footsteps,
We are helping to carry your cross. Amen.

Song: 'When I Needed a Neighbour' *(New Orbit)*

Picture: *Jesus crucified.* This is the last and worst suffering and contains all the others: he is in terrible bodily pain, people go on mocking him, and he feels so lonely that it seems even God has forsaken him. He suffered the very worst that men could do.

Reading: Mark 15.22-39

Prayer: Lord Jesus, you have known
The worst pain it is possible to suffer.
You have felt
The worst things that human beings do to each other,
The weight of all the wrongs in the world.
You share our pain
At all the hurtful things that are done to us;
And we cause you pain
By all the hurtful things that we do to others.
But even in the midst
Of your pain on the cross
You forgave the soldiers who had nailed you there,
You comforted the thief who turned to you for help,
You looked down with loving eyes
To comfort those who loved you.

You look at us now with loving eyes.
Everything we are and
Everything we have
Comes to us from God our Father
Through you.
You love us more than we can possibly imagine.
Thank you for your great love for us. Amen.

Song: 'Lord of the Dance' *(New Orbit)*

Closing Remarks: Jesus is laid in the tomb. But the song we have just sung has told us that the story doesn't finish here. For the next instalment, come on Sunday!

Closing Prayers: Thank you, Lord Jesus Christ, for all the benefits and blessings which you have given to us, for all the pain and insults which you have borne for us. O most merciful Redeemer, Friend and Brother, may we know you more clearly, love you more dearly, and follow you more nearly, day by day. Amen. *(Richard of Chichester)*

FROM DARK TO BRIGHT

A simple visual aid for Good Friday devised by Alan Beck

The following visual aid could be used in many ways, but was originally used as the basis of the lesson here described. Everyone was given an envelope (see end of article).

It is Good Friday, the church is bare. There is only the cross on the altar, but this shines splendid amongst the bare surroundings. The bare church stands for all the sad things that happened on Good Friday, but the cross shines because Jesus made that sad day into *good* Friday and changed the cross from something standing for pain and death into our glorious Christian badge reminding us how much God loves us all. To-day we have come to think about this and to thank God for his love in Jesus Christ.

The scene on Calvary—there were three crosses, not one, and on the other crosses were thieves. They could have been any two people, because every one of us is a thief—as we shall see.

We look again at an old story we find in Genesis 3. 'Once upon a time' God made a lovely garden. It was so lovely God wanted to share it so that others could enjoy it with him. So he made Man. They would work together as friends and partners, creating beautiful things, then 'in the cool of the evening' they would walk round the garden enjoying it all. Man was given everything he needed, but was asked not to touch one tree. That meant trusting God to know what was best. But of course the fruit of that tree became the one thing he wanted. He took without asking, indeed knowing he had been asked not to. He stole from his best friend *(the worst possible kind of stealing)* and couldn't look God in the face. He felt that a barrier had come between himself and God.

We then discussed how 'Adam', being the Hebrew word for Man, really stands for 'everybody'. Every child knows the temptation to take something just because it is forbidden and both parent and child are conscious of an invisible barrier which comes between them when the child disobeys. The child hides behind hands or curtain or in bedroom. 'What mischief have you been up to?'

Every one of us is Adam because God has made us and all the world. So everything belongs to God. As soon as we say 'that is mine' we forget that it is really God's. God made us, and as soon as we say 'my life is my own and I am going to do what I want to do', then we are stealing from God, and that invisible barrier comes across which makes it hard for us to think about God and so we feel that we had better keep our distance from him.

We now start on the visual aid and, assuming God is at the top of the page and we are at the bottom, we stick a broad dark line across the card, representing the division between God and Man. (This makes the crossbar of the cross.)

We now go on to see that when we fall out with God, we immediately start falling out with each other. So Adam and Eve begin to argue and set up barriers between each other (symbolised by the fig-leaf clothing). It isn't long before arguments lead to blows and bloodshed (Cain and Abel). So it is in our own experience at home and at school. As soon as we start to think 'that's mine', we start fearing that someone might take it from us. We must hide it away. We start wanting what others have got, just because they have it and we haven't. Arguments take place over what belongs to me. Things get 'pinched' from us at school. People steal other people's property, even their liberty. We pick on the things which are different about people as an opportunity for teasing.

A dark and dismal division comes between us. So we put the dark vertical division on the visual aid. The result is a dark, gloomy cross. (At this point we had a break and sang a hymn.)

Now, after working on our visual aid in sombre colours, we use bright colours, for we come to what Jesus did on Good Friday.

The whole purpose of Christ's incarnation was to break through that barrier dividing earth from heaven, to bring us out of the shadows where we have been hiding from God and into the sunshine of his love, to be re-united with God who loves us and wants us to come back and trust him again. God is like a loving father stretching out his arm to welcome his prodigal son back home. Jesus taught us to use a word for God that no-one had ever dared to use before, the ordinary Jewish child's name for Daddy—'Abba'. It is much the same in our language, dadda, pappa, being the easiest and simplest sound for a child to make. The cross shows us how much our heavenly Father loves us and longs for us. It is like a bridge over that barrier of separation.

We put in a bright vertical strip on top of the dark.

Jesus came to stretch out his hands in love to all men and bring them together again. Jesus stretched out his hands on the cross to unite us in one great family. So now we put in the bright horizontal strip which cuts across that dark vertical barrier between man and man. (We now have a bright red cross in the middle of our larger dark cross.)

Now the visual aid is finished and we see how something dark and gloomy has been transformed into something bright and beautiful. We won't try to put it into an envelope or pocket or handbag but will carry it home for all to see. We are not ashamed of the cross and we want people to be reminded of the cross on Good Friday. We will display it in our front room window when we get home.

Details of the Visual Aid

(Precise dimensions can be varied so long as the general effect is maintained.)

For each child or family prepare:

Stiff piece of card 17 cm × 10 cm.

Envelope containing

one brown gummed paper strip 23 mm × 76 mm
one brown gummed paper strip 23 mm × 127 mm
one red gummed paper strip 12 mm × 76 mm
one red gummed paper strip 12 mm × 127 mm

I used pale blue board duplicating paper which gives four cards per sheet, and Jollycraft Gummed Paper Squares (20 cm × 20 cm), the dark brown and bright red sheets. Each brown sheet makes eight sets and each red one twice as many. A guillotine is virtually essential and it is easiest to cut with the gummed side uppermost.

I duplicated the outline of the cross on the card, but this is hardly necessary. Envelopes can be collected afterwards for further use.

NOTES ON A STUDY OF A CROSS

This outline of a sermon by the Rev. R. J. Goodchild was sent to us (with his permission) by a parishioner who felt that 'Together' readers might find teaching ideas within it

In our increasingly complicated world there is a need for simple symbols which everyone can understand. Road signs are now universal, industry uses simple trade marks, political parties use colours and every new movement adopts a sign. The swastika, the Red Cross, the hammer and sickle, the Olympic flag, the clenched fist, British Rail sign, EEC, all are examples of signs that tell us in shorthand what they mean.

The simplest sign of all is the Christian Cross. It is the first shape a baby draws, it is used when an old person can no longer sign his name, but like all the best symbols and signs it has depths of meaning behind its simplicity.

Let us look with fresh eyes at the Christian symbol and see that behind that simplicity there is much to learn.

What does it look like?

It looks like a sign-post. It offers us two ways on the path of life. The path of self and the path to God. We have to choose, there is no middle way. It challenges us to make up our mind.

Look at it again and it looks like a letter T—T for truth. Only here can the truth be found about God, about man, about life, about death, about suffering, about purpose.

Look at it again and it is an I crossed out—We are naturally selfish and we have to learn to live with one another and to serve one another. 'I' is no longer the centre of my life—the Cross is.

Look at it again and it looks like a man with open arms. This is what Christianity is. It is not a set of rules, it is not an ideology—it is an invitation. Come to me, says Jesus, and I will give you my love, my protection and my care. No one ever need feel lonely if they look at the Cross.

Look at it again and it looks like a banner. Held high it gives us a cause to follow, a set of principles to fight for, a marching band to join, a crusade to take part in, a challenge to the young and a banner raised against evil, injustice, false values and uselessness of life. It leads us into war against an enemy around us and within us.

Look at it again and it looks like a sword. A weapon with which to fight. St. Paul says: 'Our fight is not against human foes but against cosmic powers, against the authorities and potentates of this dark world, against the superhuman forces of evil.'

Look at it once more and it is made up of a vertical and horizontal line. The vertical is firmly embedded in this world, for Christianity is not some airy-fairy vision, but rooted and grounded in human experience—it is incarnate. But the vertical line leads us up to the heavenly places and guides our minds up to God. The horizontal line reaches out to the world—for Christianity is not just a personal faith, it is a corporate one reaching out to others. And notice that the horizontal is supported by the vertical. A man may have a strong social conscience and say 'I do not go to church but I serve others'—but without the vertical dimension of worship, the horizontal falls to the ground and is weakened.

These two lines remind us of our Lord's two great principles of life: reverence God and respect others. All there in the symbol of the Cross.

Perhaps you can see other meanings as you look at it? A pair of balances giving us a balanced view of life, a sign of baptism that we carry everywhere and always invisibly on our foreheads, a sign of the Trinity—but finally let us notice one more thing.

It is empty. No figure of Christ hangs on it. We do not worship a dead figure of history but a living Lord. Jesus experienced the Cross and overcame it. We too have our crosses to bear, our weak human bodies, our faults of character, our worries, responsibilities, failures—but in the end the Cross is empty, for Christ is alive and offers us eternal life if we follow him past the Cross to the other side.

A simple sign with endless depths of meaning. Christianity is very simple, a child can understand it, but it has depths that no one can fully understand or master. May we see the Holy Cross as a symbol, in our homes, round our necks, at our prayers and look at it with fresh eyes to see some of its meanings. I have pointed out twelve meanings—I wonder how many you will remember?

'LORD, TEACH US. . .'

A three-hours' service for Good Friday, devised for children by Margaret Williams

The theme is based on the following prayer:

'By the prayers of Jesus, Lord, teach us how to pray;
By the gifts of Jesus, Lord, teach us how to give;
By the toils of Jesus, Lord, teach us how to work;
By the love of Jesus, Lord, teach us how to love;
By the cross of Jesus, Lord, teach us how to live.'

The three hours were divided into five sessions, each session being based on one line of the prayer. There was a short break after the third session when the children had a drink and a hot-cross bun.

If possible and if space allows it, each child should have two places—a working place at a table where he or she is going to make a book during the three hours, and a place in the centre of the hall where the talk and worship sessions take place. It is also good to have a signal, such as music being played on the piano or tape-recorder, which will indicate to the children when it is time to leave their tables and come together. This avoids too many instructions being given during the time, and children respond to this very well. (Even if they have not completed the page they are doing, they will be able to catch up later.) At their tables the children will need pens or pencils, crayons or felt-tipped pens, scissors, paste and a Bible. At their other places, children will need hymn books.

Session 1 'By the prayers of Jesus, Lord, teach us how to pray'

The talk is about Jesus at prayer. Reference is made to Mark 1.35 and it is emphasised that Jesus was constantly in the habit of praying. Someone reads Matthew 6.5-15 to show what Jesus said about prayer.

Let the children think about the pattern prayer which Jesus gave us—which bit do they consider most important for them? Then the talk goes to the second phrase 'Lord, teach us how to pray' and we think of our own prayer life—when did it begin? How does it grow? What different kinds of prayer are there? We tell the children about prayers of praise, prayers of thanks and prayers of asking. This is then followed by a worship session.

WORSHIP

Hymn: 'Father, hear the prayer we offer.'

Prayer: 'O Lord, who helped the disciples when they asked "Lord, teach us to pray", we ask you to help us now that we might know how to pray.'

The Lord's Prayer.

Leader: 'By the prayers of Jesus . . .'

Children: 'Lord, teach us how to pray.'

All sing Verse 1 of the special hymn (see page 80).

Then the children proceed to their tables to work on pages 1 and 2 of their books.

Session 2 'By the gifts of Jesus, Lord, teach us how to give'

Here the talk centres on what Jesus gave to us—first, what he gave up as the Son of God to come to live on earth. To do this was something tremendous but when he came there was no room for him to be born in a house. Recall the nativity story very briefly. Jesus gave up so much for us—how much ought we to give for Jesus? 'Lord, teach us how to give.' Everyone who is a Christian can give something because we all have something to give.

We give up our time to doing things for Jesus; we give money to help and further his work and we should also give our talents too. We all possess talents or gifts and no matter how small and insignificant they are if we offer them to Jesus, he can make our smallest efforts worthwhile.

A reader reads John 6.1-14. Comment on this story—the fact that the boy offered only five loaves and two fish but Jesus could make more of them; the boy had to offer them first. It is like this with our gifts; we have to offer them and God can make more of them.

WORSHIP

Hymn: 'Take my life and let it be
Consecrated Lord, to Thee.'

'O Lord, we thank you for the talents you have given us—we are all different and you want us to offer all the variety of gifts we have to you. Show us ways of using our talents to do your work in the world.'

Leader: 'By the gifts of Jesus . . .'

Children: 'Lord, teach us how to give.'

Verse 2 of the special hymn.

Session 3 'By the toils of Jesus, Lord, teach us how to work'

The aim of this session is to show that Jesus did God's work continually, not just on Sabbath days but every day and we, as Christians, should try to do the same. Reference is made to the physical toils of Jesus, as in Luke 8.1, when his travelling is mentioned; Luke 6.19, when people crowded around him for healing and 'power' went out from him; Luke 4.28, when the crowds threatened him. However, Jesus still did God's work, no matter what the cost to himself.

'Lord, teach us how to work.' From the example of Jesus we can learn that being a Christian is a full-time job—we are Christians for seven days a week and not just on Sundays. The verse 'Christ has no hands but our hands' can be read to children and we talk about the help of God's Holy Spirit and the increasing part that he can take in our lives as we grow, if we allow him to.

WORSHIP

Hymn: 'O Jesus, I have promised.'

'Lord Jesus, we thank you for the example of work well done. May we do all the tasks before us to the best of our ability and may we remember to do things as you would want us to do, with your help.'

Leader: 'By the toils of Jesus . . .'

Children: 'Lord, teach us how to work'

Verse 3 of special hymn.

Session 4 'By the love of Jesus, Lord, teach us how to love'

To show the love of Jesus, the story of healing of the leper in Luke 5.12-16 is read, bringing out that in that healing Jesus touched him (he need not have done this in order to heal him) to show he loved him.

'Lord, teach us how to love.' Here the story of the Good Samaritan is told to show how Jesus taught people about loving one's neighbour. (Because this story was fairly well known by the children, it was read from the Bible and then they recounted it by answering questions about it.)

WORSHIP

Hymn: 'O Lord, all the world belongs to you.'

'Lord Jesus, we thank you for your great love for us.
Help us to love others, even when we find it hard to do so.'

Leader: 'By the love of Jesus . . .'

Children: 'Lord, teach us how to love.'

Verse 4 of special hymn.

Session 5 'By the cross of Jesus, teach us how to live'

For this session the story of Good Friday and Easter Day is told. The emphasis should be that this is the summing-up of all that we have been thinking about, for on the cross Jesus made the perfect prayer when he prayed for those who nailed him there; he made the perfect gift—the giving of himself totally—and he showed perfect love.

'Lord, teach us how to live.' The verse about Simon from Cyrene is read from Matthew 27.32—as he carried the cross so do we, but ours is an invisible one made on our foreheads at our baptism.

The only activity work, done immediately after this talk, is the cutting out and sticking in the books of two crosses—a purple one and a gold one. The final worship session can be taken after this activity time.

CLOSING WORSHIP

Verse 5 of special hymn.

Leader: 'By the prayers of Jesus . . .'
Children: 'Lord, teach us how to pray.'
Leader: 'By the gifts of Jesus . . .'
Children: Lord, teach us how to give . . .'
Leader: 'By the toils of Jesus . . .'
Children: 'Lord, teach us how to work.'
Leader: 'By the love of Jesus . . .'
Children: 'Lord, teach us how to love.'
Leader: 'By the cross of Jesus . . .'
Children: 'Lord, teach us how to live.'

Final hymn: 'Raise the cross.'

Special Hymn Tune: 'At the Name of Jesus' (*Thirty 20th Century Hymn Tunes,* Josef Weinberger Ltd)

1. By the prayers of Jesus,
   Teach us how to pray.
   As we look at Jesus
   He shows us the way.
   Jesus is our pattern
   We must follow him,
   Learn from him and love him,
   For he is our King.

2. By the gifts of Jesus,
   Teach us how to give.
   May we use our talents
   To help others to live.
   Jesus is our pattern,
   We must follow him,
   Learn from him and love him,
   For he is our King.

3. By the toils of Jesus,
Teach us how to work,
Doing what is right
Trying not to shirk.
Jesus is our pattern,
We must follow him,
Learn from him and love him,
For he is our King.

4. By the love of Jesus,
Teach us how to love,
Even show our friendship
To those hard to love.
Jesus is our pattern,
We must follow him,
Learn from him and love him,
For he is our King.

5. By the cross of Jesus,
Teach us how to live.
May we all, as Christians,
Learn to love and forgive.
Jesus is our pattern,
We must follow him,
Learn from him and love him,
For he is our King.

Books .

The 'books' which the children made during the activity sessions were prepared in outline beforehand and each child was given a duplicated 12-page copy. On the cover was an outline drawing of Jesus and the title, 'Let us learn from Jesus'. Their contents were as follows, all drawings being in outline to allow for colouring in.

page 1: Heading: 'By the prayers of Jesus . . .'
'Jesus prayed constantly throughout his life.'
(Drawing of praying hands.)
'Very early next morning he got up and went out. He went away to a lonely spot and remained there in prayer.' (Mark 1.35)

page 2: Heading: 'Lord, teach us how to pray.'
'Our prayer life began at our baptism.'
(Drawing of font with lit candles surrounding it.)

'As we grow, so should our prayer life. To pray is to bring things to Jesus. In this space, write a thanking prayer.'

'In this space, write an asking prayer.'

page 3: Heading: 'By the gifts of Jesus . . .'
(Drawing of Nativity—baby in manger.)
'God loved the world so much that he GAVE his only Son.' (John 3.16)

page 4: Heading: 'Lord, teach us how to give.'
'We all have various talents given to us by God for us to give back to him in service. If we offer him our talents, he can use them as he accepted and used the five loaves and two fishes.'
(Drawing of loaves and fishes.)
'Write here one thing you are good at.'

'Jesus accepts what we offer.'

page 5: Heading: 'By the toils of Jesus . . .'
'Jesus did God's work continually,'
(Drawing of party walking up winding road)
'He went journeying from town to town and village to village, proclaiming the good news of the kingdom of God.' (Luke 8.1)
(Drawing of reaching out hands.)
'And everyone in the crowd was trying to touch him, because power went out from him and cured them all.' (Luke 6.19)
'And so must we.'

page 6: Heading: 'Lord, teach us how to work.'
'Christ has no hands but our hands
To do his work today;
Christ has no feet but our feet
To lead men in his way;
Christ has no lips but our lips
To tell men why he died;
Christ has no help but our help
To win men on his side.'

(Drawing of boy and girl kneeling to receive laying-on of hands.)
'To do this we are helped by God's Holy Spirit and our strength renewed.'

page 7: Heading: 'By the love of Jesus . . .'
'The love of Jesus knew no bounds.'
(Space for child's drawing of healing)

'Jesus stretched out his hand and touched him.' (Luke 5.13)

page 8: Heading: 'Lord, teach us how to love.'
'Jesus said, "Love your neighbour as yourself."
'What story did Jesus tell to show who is our neighbour?'

'In this story, which man was the good neighbour?'

'Put a tick by the people in this list who are neighbours to you:
Your friend
A boy in your class at school
An old lady who lives two streets away
The person who lives next door to you
A girl you often see on your way to school
A boy who is always trying to quarrel with you.'

page 9: Heading: 'By the cross of Jesus . . .'
'Father, forgive them; they do not know what they are doing.' (Luke 23.34)

'On Good Friday, this is what Jesus did—
He made the perfect prayer.
He made the perfect gift.
He showed perfect love.
AND HE DID THIS FOR US.'

page 10: Heading: 'Lord, teach us how to live.'
'On their way out, they met a man from Cyrene, Simon by name, and pressed him into service to carry his cross.' (Matthew 27.32)

'This cross is the sign of victory. Jesus has won—he has conquered evil for *always*.'

The child could write his name, church, etc., on the back cover.

WHAT JESUS SAID

Another of Margaret Williams' three-hour activities for children, using home-made work-books

The theme for this three-hour activity was 'What Jesus said then and what Jesus says now'. The three hours were divided into five sessions and the following sayings of Jesus were taken:

(1) Follow me
(2) Be still
(3) You must love God and love your neighbour
(4) Forgive them
(5) You will receive power

Each session consisted of a talk by the leader followed by worship. Then the children went to tables to work on a page in their work-books. Each child had a copy of the Gospel according to St. Luke, the *Good News by Luke* version, so they were able to find the Bible references by page numbers and all follow them in the same versions. The illustrations in their work-books were also taken from *Good News by Luke.* On each double page in their books, the left-hand page was about the incident recorded in the Bible, the right-hand page suggested how we can carry out what Jesus is saying to us today. The pictures were in outline to allow for colouring in, and spaces were provided to allow for the children's own writing or drawing.

Session 1—Jesus said, 'Follow me'

Refer to the game 'Follow the leader'. If felt appropriate, this could be played for a few minutes. What does 'follow me' mean? Refer to the call of the fishermen and to the call of Levi. The children can find both these stories and follow while they are read out and referred to. Ask how many disciples Jesus chose and whether he asked anyone else to follow him. Look at Luke chapter 10 verse 1, pointing out the fact that although Jesus called many people to be his followers, he didn't ask them all to give up everything—some gave up their work to follow him, some followed him in their everyday work.

It is just like this today. Jesus is saying 'Follow me' to us today, and he says it in the same way as he did years ago. He calls some people, such as monks and nuns, to give up everything (elaborate). He calls some people to dedicate their working lives to him. He calls *all* of us to be his disciples. How can we do this? First he wants us to show God's love in our lives, secondly he wants us to tell others about him.

Worship Hymn: 'When Jesus walked in Galilee' (*Sing Hosanna,* Holmes McDougall)

'O Lord, you said "Follow me" to your disciples so long ago. You are saying "Follow me" to us here today. When we are older you might want some of us to follow you in a very particular way. You might want us to give up our everyday work to follow you. If this is so, may we have the courage to leave all for your sake. But here and now you are calling us to follow; may we be good examples of being Christian and may others see in us a little bit of you. Amen.'

Session 2—Jesus said, 'Be still'

Ask about storms: has anyone been at sea or by the sea in a storm? If felt appropriate, the children could together mime a storm—waves getting rougher and then gradually growing calm again. Read the story of Jesus stilling the storm. Let the children imagine the scene—they will all have seen storms on television. Jesus calmed the sea and the winds, and he calmed the disciples. They were afraid, frightened, they panicked and Jesus calmed them. This is the effect Jesus had on many people. Remember the donkey on Palm Sunday? The donkey did not kick or try to shake him off, Jesus made him calm. Jesus has this effect on people today. Sometimes we are frightened, sometimes we are afraid, sometimes we panic—but if we pray, Jesus says to us 'Be still'. It is when we do not stop and talk to Jesus that we go on being afraid.

There are times when we need other people, there are times when we need to be alone. Talking to God is just like that—there are times when it is good to do this with others, when we worship and pray together in church, and there are times when it is good to talk to God on our own.

Worship Hymn: 'Lord Jesus Christ, you have come to us' *(Sing Hosanna)*

'Still, still, Jesus is here
Still, still, angels are near.
Jesus we come to thee,
Standing so quietly,
Now we are close to thee,
Jesus is here.'

'Help us, Lord, to be still and quiet. There are times when we are so busy that we forget all about you but you do not forget about us. For this we thank you, Lord.'

Session 3—Jesus said, 'You must love God and love your neighbour'

Talk about why we should love God—children may suggest that it might be because God created us and all the world and that God loves us. Jesus said that you cannot love God without loving your neighbour. Children follow in their gospels while someone reads the story of the Good Samaritan. If felt appropriate, a group of children could mime this story during the reading. Invite comments on the story by asking such questions as: 'Do you think the people who passed by might have had a good reason for not stopping and offering assistance?' We often put off doing things for others because it would interfere with our plans. Who is *our* neighbour? It is anyone who is in need. How can we help? Show posters from Christian Aid and describe what the money that we collect for Christian Aid can do. It can send trained people overseas to help; it can pay for engineering projects to bring water to remote villages, etc. Elaborate according to the posters which are available. (They are obtainable from Education Dept., Christian Aid, 240/250 Ferndale Road, London SW9 8BH)

Worship Hymn: 'When I needed a neighbour, were you there?' *(Sing Hosanna)*

'There are many people who need us as neighbours and as friends. May we not miss any opportunities that come our way to be a friend to someone in need. May we help not only the people we like, but also the people we find it difficult to like. Amen.'

Session 4—Jesus said, 'Forgive them'

Tell the story of Good Friday, stressing the fact that Jesus was able to say 'Father, forgive them for they know not what they do' about the people who were killing him.

Jesus says to us today, 'Forgive one another'. Try to find a topical story to illustrate someone forgiving someone else. A good one is that of Corrie ten Boom meeting, years after the war, one of the men who had been a guard at the concentration camp where she was imprisoned. It is retold in *This is the Life* (CIO).

Worship Hymn: 'O Lord, all the world belongs to you' (*27 20th Century Hymns,* Josef Weinberger)

'We remember how you were able to say 'Forgive them' when you were dying on the cross on that first Good Friday. You could say this because you loved people; if only we would love people half as much as you did, then we would be able to forgive people more often than we do and the world would be a better place. Help us to forgive others, Lord.'

Session 5—Jesus said, 'You will receive power'

Tell the story of Easter and the Ascension, emphasising the fact that after Easter the disciples had met together in the Upper Room and that although they went to the Temple, they did not preach or teach the people. Then tell the story of the first Whitsunday, emphasising the difference that the gift of God's Holy Spirit made to the disciples. They preached to and taught the people of Jerusalem without being afraid. They were able to heal people and they were full of the joy and the love of God.

We too can be helped by God's Holy Spirit, for the promise made to the disciples was made to us too. We can tell others about Jesus and can do so without being afraid, and we can help in making people whole in body, mind and spirit.

Final Worship Hymn: 'Raise the Cross' *(27 20th Century Hymns)*

'Lord Jesus, we thank you for your great love for us and for all you are willing to do for us, although we are so unworthy. May our lives shine forth with your love. Amen.'

THE WINDS OF SPRING

A poem for Easter
by Hilda Rostron

The winds of Spring blow shadows out of sight.
The dawning sun spills gold into the empty tomb
and Easter triumphs over Winter's tears
with radiant flowers dispelling gloom.

The winds of Spring melted the frozen bough;
behind us are the days when no sun shone;
the time of doubt and pain forgotten now.
He lives! Death from the grave is gone.

The winds of Spring welcome returning life;
silence is broken by the songs of birds;
mourning is changed to deep enduring faith.
Man's tongue finds hard to turn it into words.

The winds of Spring bring proof to satisfy,
revealing glory in a garden fair.
Rejoice, rejoice! Let Christian men find voice,
salute the Risen Lord whose feet walk there.

Still blow the winds of Spring
leaf, bird and flower sing
my heart its praises bring . . .
Alleluia!

RIDING

J. A. Thomas

Who's that riding down the street, On a donkey on a donkey?
Clothed in white from head to feet, Riding on a donkey.

Chorus

Hail! hail! it's Jesus Christ, Donkey riding, donkey riding,
Hail! hail! it's Jesus Christ, Riding on a donkey.

2. On this joyful Sunday morn
   We are glad that Christ was born
   For he's bringing hope to man
   Riding on a donkey.

   Chorus

3. Though it happened long ago
   Donkey riding, donkey riding,
   This Palm Sunday, we will go
   Riding on a donkey.

   Chorus

4. Soon he'll die upon a cross
   When mankind will feel his loss
   But he has his triumph now
   Riding on a donkey.

   Chorus

5. So today, with palms and songs
   Born again, forgiving wrongs
   He brings hope to us each year
   Riding on a donkey.

   Chorus

Who's that rid-ing down the street, On a donkey on a donkey,
Clothed in white from head to feet, Rid-ing on a don - key.
Chorus
Hail! hail! it's Jes - us Christ Don-key rid-ing donkey rid-ing
Hail! hail! it's Jes - us Christ, Rid - ing on a don - key.

PALM SUNDAY

A poem for two or many voices, by drama teacher Claude Holmes

The people are waiting,
Surging through the square,
Butting down the dusty alleyways,
Toe-tramping, shin-kicking, grumbling.
'Who d'you think you're shoving?
Just you wait!
  Just you wait.
    Just
      you
        wait.'

'Why are we waiting?
What are we waiting for?
  Who?'

'He's coming!

'Who?'

That's it—who.

Dr. Who, the Time Lord to put it right.
Magician to put us all wise.
All-speaking Mr. Spock.
A new Arthur to right the wrongs with a strong right arm.
A Lenin, Churchill, Castro
To scatter the dust of our enemies
Over the slippery path we tread.
He'll come. He must.
  It can't go on like this.

'He's coming!
Look now—Coming. He is.'

No. It's the Romans. It's the army. Motorcade.
No. It's only a man on a donkey—
  Gentle-looking beast.
  No war horse, prancing charger.
  No tanks.

'Oh, him.'

Never mind, he'll do.
A figure to cheer for lack of other thrills.
  He's nuts, of course,
  But give him a cheer for trying.
We can afford a palm leaf or two
Before the authorities catch up with him.
  Breach of the peace.

Look at their faces—the Establishment!
Makes a diversion, and we're not involved,
Not really.

Hosanna, You can have that for free.

  Hosanna, Hosanna!

AFTER EASTER, A NEW TERM

A meditation for Assembly
by Claude Holmes

So you're starting a new term.

Seems a shame to start again in spring-time.
The holidays are always much too short.

The classroom smells of furniture polish;
Stronger than the new-cut grass on the Square.
Everybody's voice is louder,
Louder than you can remember;
But your best friend is speaking to you again
For the time being.

Maybe last term wasn't quite so hot.
Report left much to be desired.
Exhortation battles with apathies and fears;
And examinations cast
Sharper shadows in the summer sun
Than they ever did in the fogs of November
Or the weeping skies of Lent.

Teachers, too—
Packing a two-pint syllabus into a one-pint pot;
Sharpening red pencils
And polishing blackboards.
Watching the calendar in the Examination Hall.

It all begins again.
Seems such a shame when the commercials
Give promise of lazy days in the sun.
  Months away.
It's all begun again.

God began again in springtime.
After the slow despair of a Friday morning,
And the spring rain of Mary's tears,
Hope sprang green in an upper room,
And there were three for supper at Emmaus.
  Starting a new term.

THE GOOD FRIDAY GARDEN

Easter Gardens are a popular visual aid—but a Good Friday Garden? Isobel Galilee describes how one came into being in her church

Easter gardens still have a lot of appeal—as a simple 'visual aid', a symbol of our Easter joy, with its empty tomb and spring flowers. In our parish in the last few years we have expanded the idea a little further, I think, than most, and our Garden is a focus for our Good Friday Family Service, which is growing in popularity, as well as for our Easter Day celebrations.

I believe it is a good thing to encourage children to come to church on Good Friday, as it is easier for them to understand the joy of Easter if they have first experienced something of the solemnity of Good Friday, with the church bare, the altar stripped, perhaps the crucifixes covered, and the general atmosphere of waiting which seems to characterise this day. For them, as for adult Christians, the story of Easter should begin with the Cross. Yet what can we offer them on such a day? Many parents, I think, shy away from the idea of bringing children to church on Good Friday, fearing something too gloomy and solemn, perhaps even morbid.

A few years ago we experimented with a short service followed by an invitation to the children to help make an Easter Garden. This was reasonably successful, but we found it difficult to find enough jobs for our number of keen children to do in a small area. Before the following Good Friday we looked at the idea again. We still wanted the children to have a hand in the making of the Garden; on the other hand an already completed garden, with its atmosphere of mystery, could have a powerful effect on children's imaginations. We evolved a fruitful compromise.

Every year since then our Garden has been made on a trestle table by the chancel steps on Maundy Thursday. (A trestle table, especially if you lack an obvious place for your Easter Garden in the church, has the advantage that the Garden is portable, above floor level, and can be placed where it can most easily be seen.) The basis is of two 'hills', the larger for Calvary, the smaller for the tomb, made from papier-mâché stiffened underneath with chicken wire. This landscape is painted in greens and browns and covers about two-thirds of the table surface, the edges of it merging into the sand, covered with damp moss, which covers the rest of the table. On Good Friday morning, the hill of Calvary is bare, the tomb stands empty. Apart from the moss, the only foliage is symbolically stark—teazle heads, thorny dead-looking twigs (butcher's broom) have been stuck here and there, giving the effect of a desolate landscape, reinforced by a backcloth of black clouds and streaks of lightning.

During our service the story of Christ's crucifixion, death and burial is told in simple terms by the Vicar (or by someone else, perhaps with the aid of readings) and at the appropriate moments individual children from the congregation are invited to place the central cross on Calvary, then the other two crosses, and a Roman soldier nearby. (Our Roman soldiers are very tiny and come from a plastic set sold in toy shops, which also includes a chariot and horses. They could equally well be handmade, as are our crosses.) The Descent from the Cross is symbolised by the placing of a ladder against the central cross, and the Burial by small pieces of linen bandage being put in the tomb. Finally the stone is placed over the entrance and more Roman soldiers are set to guard it. Somewhere in the landscape is set a lonely donkey—who brought Christ into Jerusalem on Palm Sunday.

This simple 'heart' to our service is suitable even for quite young children and involves about a dozen children from the congregation. At the end of the service there is always a rush to look more closely at the miniature landscape which tells its own story so effectively.

On Easter Day the black clouds are replaced by a sunny backcloth of blue skies and white clouds. The 'dead' trees have given way to twigs coming into leaf and spikes of green rosemary and yellow forsythia, while the hills are dotted with the bright heads of 'everlasting' flowers. The sad donkey has been joined by a host of vaguely appropriate animals who gambol on the hillsides—goats, rabbits, sheep and a few pigs, 'borrowed' from farm sets. The stone has, of course, been removed from the door of the tomb and the soldiers have gone, to be replaced by two small figures (shepherds from a nativity set) who gaze wonderingly into the empty tomb. As a final touch, the Sunday school children, when they come into church as usual halfway through the Parish Communion, bring their own bunches of spring flowers which are placed in tiny jars (paste jars or baby-food tins) hidden in the moss.

If the moss and sand are regularly sprinkled with water, our Garden stays fresh and beautiful for at least a week after Easter as a living symbol of the Easter story—but equally important for us, as a 'visual aid' or what you will, is our strange, bleak, desolate Garden for Good Friday.

A SIMPLE FORM OF PASSOVER

Teaching about the Last Supper is often introduced by a study of Passover. Sylvia Ross has found this simplified form of the rite to be a helpful resource for teachers of 9s-13s

Blessing of lights [*candles lighted*]

Blessed are you, O God, King of all creation, who created the stars as lamps of fire.

Blessing of wine [*cup passed round*]

Blessed are you, O Lord our God, King of all creation, creator of the fruit of the vine. Blessed are you, O Lord, who chose us to be your People. You have given us times of joy and gladness, this feast of Passover, the time of our freedom, a celebration in memory of our escape from Egypt. Blessed are you, O Lord, who kept us safe, and brought us to this night.

Blessing of bitter herbs

Blessed are you, O God, King of all creation, creator of the fruit of the earth.

Recital [*breaking the bread*]

This is the bread of sorrow which our ancestors ate in the land of Egypt. Let all who are hungry come in and eat. Let all who are in want come in and celebrate the Passover with us.

Questions: Why is this night different from all other nights?

Why do we eat unleavened bread and bitter herbs?

Answer: We were slaves of Pharaoh in Egypt, and the Lord our God brought us forth from there with a mighty hand and outstretched arm. And if the Holy One had not set our fathers free from Egypt, then we, and our children, and our children's children would have been slaves of Pharaoh in Egypt.

Litany: Response: We would have thought it enough

If the Lord had brought us through the Sea of Reeds, and not led us through the desert:

If he had led us through the desert, and not fed us with the manna:

If he had fed us with the manna, and not given us water from the rock:

If he had given us water from the rock, and not made us his own People:

If he had made us his own People, and not given us the Promised Land.

Answer [*continued*] The memory of the escape of our forefathers from Egypt will never fail to inspire us with new courage, and the symbols of this Festival always help to strengthen our faith in God, the Saviour of the ill-treated. So we must learn the meaning of these three symbols: the Passover sacrifice, the unleavened bread and the bitter herbs.

This lamb bone [*hold up bone*], symbol of the Passover sacrifice, reminds us how our forefathers offered a lamb to God on the night when he led them out of slavery in Egypt, and how they put the blood on their doorposts and were saved from the plague which destroyed the Egyptians.

This unleavened bread [*lift bread*] reminds us that, when our forefathers escaped from Egypt, there was no time to wait for the yeast to make the dough rise, so that they had to carry unleavened dough with them on their journey.

This bitter herb [*point to herbs*] reminds us of the bitterness of our forefathers' lives in Egypt, when the Egyptians treated them as slaves.

[*This Answer can be expanded by the teacher, according to the age of the children. The Questions are traditionally asked by the youngest child.*]

Each of us must enter into this celebration as though each of us had escaped from Egypt: it was not only our fathers that the Holy One—may he be praised—redeemed; he redeemed us with them. We should therefore sing praises and give thanks to him who has done all this for us. He has brought us from slavery to freedom, from sorrow to joy, from darkness to light.

Blessing of bread [*said by all*]

Blessed are you, O Lord our God, King of all creation, who brings forth bread from the earth. [*bread eaten; herbs distributed and eaten*]

Leader: Let us give thanks to the Lord our God

All: It is right to give him thanks and praise. Blessed are you, O Lord our God, King of all creation, who feed the whole world by your love and kindness. Because of your faithful care, we have had enough food, and we believe that you will always provide for us.

Leader: O God, the God of our forefathers, remember us as you remembered them, so that we may find freedom, grace, mercy, life and peace on this Feast.

All: Amen.

Leader: O give thanks to the Lord, for he is good, and his great love is without end.

Blessing of wine [*cup passed round*]

Blessed are you, O Lord our God, King of all creation, creator of the fruit of the vine.

Psalm 135: 'O give thanks to the Lord, for he is good'.

[You may like to use the setting by Gelineau to be found in *Twenty-Four Psalms and a Canticle,* published by The Grail, 125 Waxwell Lane, Pinner, Middx.]

Note: Teachers may find the chapter 'Re-living the Passover' in *Understanding your Jewish Neighbour,* by Myer Domnitz (Lutterworth Educational) to be a useful source of additional background information and pictures.

GIVE US A SIGN!

A Course for Holy Week by Christopher Owens

By and large, Holy Week passes without touching the greater part of our congregation, and as habits are more easily formed in young people than in adults, I decided to start with a project aimed at children, and hoped that the idea would spread.

I was greatly helped and encouraged by the magazine *Together* and its associated publications, and also by the *Celebration* series published by Galliard.

At the beginning of Lent our Brownies, Cubs and three junior Sunday school classes chose one emblem of the Passion, and set about making a centre-piece in whatever medium seemed best to them: for example, the Brownies made a cockerel in collage with pink feathers and orange tissue paper.

In Passion Week each Brownie, Cub and Sunday school child was given a duplicated booklet, 'My Holy Week'. The inside covers had the order of Service, which was the same each day.

Song: 'Jesus is a friend of mine' (114, *Sound of Living Waters,* Hodder & Stoughton)

Prayer of Confession:

Lord, here is your cross.
Your cross! As if it were your cross!
You had no cross, and you came to get ours; and all through your life, and all along the way to Calvary, you took upon yourself, one by one, the sins of the world. I manage very well, Lord, to pity your sufferings.
But to weep for my own sins, that's another matter.

Priest: Lord, I am not perfect.
All: Teach me that I am not perfect.
Priest: Lord, I am sorry for my failings.
All: Teach me to hate my sin.
Priest: Lord, my sin hurts your heart of love.
All: Teach me by your love.
Priest: Lord, I long to be perfect.
All: Draw me by your love.

Address

Prayer of Self-Offering:

Lord, you had nothing left but your coat.
You were fond of it: your Mother had woven it for you.
But this too had to go.
Only one thing is necessary, Lord: your cross.
It is ready. Made to measure.

Priest: Lord, you have given me work to do.

All: Jesus, fill every act of mine.

Priest: Lord, you have given me people to love.

All: Jesus, make my loving strong and true.

Priest: Lord, you have given me life.

All: Jesus, help me to share it freely and joyfully.

Hymn:

'When I survey the wondrous cross' (107 E.H. vv 1, 3, 5)

Priest: O Lord Jesus Christ, in your Cross and precious Death, your love has conquered the world:

All: Save us and help us, we pray.

Each day has a double page in the book, illustrating the Emblem, and with either a picture to draw or colour, or some simple written exercise. The illustrations were often copied from the wonderfully clear yet simple line drawings in *Good News for Modern Man* (Fontana).

Monday 'A Moment of Weakness' THE COCKEREL

In telling the story of Peter's denial, stress the humanity of Peter, and Jesus' understanding and forgiving look.

Tuesday 'Our God's Crown' THE CROWN OF THORNS

After a discussion of the rat race and the kind of crowns men chase after, contrast Christ our God and his acceptance of the crown offered to him, and what he made of it.

Wednesday 'A Lasting Impression' ST. VERONICA'S KERCHIEF

Veronica's kindness made a lasting impression on the heart of God. A prayer, slightly adapted, from *Everyman's Way to the Cross* (Ave Maria Press):

Christ: Can you be brave enough to wipe my bloody face?

Man: Lord, where is your face?

Christ: At home when eyes fill up with tears,
at work when tension rises, on playgrounds,
in slums, in courts and hospitals and jails,
wherever suffering exists—my face is

there. And I look for you to wipe away
my blood and tears.

Man: Lord, what you ask is hard: it calls for
courage and self-sacrifice like yours.
Lord, love in me, act in me, live in me!

Thursday 'Take the Blame' THE SCOURGE

When things go wrong, it's hard to take the blame, even when it really is your fault. (The children were asked to write a prayer for people who cause trouble and pain to others.)

Friday 'Man can Build . . .' HAMMER AND NAILS

. . . and man can destroy . . . everything, except God's love and forgiveness.

The services were at 6.30 p.m. on Monday to Friday in Holy Week, and none lasted over twenty minutes. The children gathered in a semicircle, in front of the Emblem of the day. At the end of each service, they were asked to leave church quietly, taking their books with them, so they could complete that day's page when they got home.

We began with a fairly small group of children, but by the end of the week we counted over 30 children and a good sprinkling of adults. At its next meeting the Church Committee asked that a similar course be provided on other suitable occasions, and that they should be advertised as for all ages. So the Holy Week course was followed by one during the week before our Patronal Festival, based on incidents in the life of St. Francis, and another for the week before Christmas.

A CROSSWORD WALK FOR GOOD FRIDAY

Exercise for mind and body is brought together by Ian Robins in this and the following activity

Ian Robins, who is vicar of a parish in Cumbria, organised two outdoor events on successive Good Fridays which were designed to enable those taking part to remember the significance of the day and, at the same time, to get out on to the fells for the first holiday of the Spring.

Before each event a small committee met several times, to organise the walk and the catering and to consider the 'religious' content of the event. They planned the route, times of starting and finishing, safety provisions, etc.; the provision of coffee, squash and hot cross buns in the hall of the parish where the walk finished; and the creation of a puzzle which would involve the devotional dimension. For the first walk this consisted of three crosswords, for adults, teenagers and children. Walkers were provided with route maps for the eight-mile course, and also with a crossword blank of the appropriate kind. At various points on the walk they found previously placed quiz questions which focused attention on the events of the Passion (in chronological order), and filled in the answers. It was stressed that the exercise was its own reward, and no prizes were offered. A charge of 30p (20p for children) was made for map, puzzle and refreshments, and profits were sent to Amnesty International. Maps were on sale in advance at local stationers, or could be purchased at the start of the walk.

Both events were widely advertised in shops and churches around two deaneries and local press and radio were notified. On the day itself some 160 people checked in; the number of complete families, including teenagers, was notable. Parties were carefully signed in, warned of difficulties and told of emergency arrangements if help was needed. They then set off, the last leaving by 11 a.m. At about 2 p.m. the catering team took over—most of the food and drink was donated, and this increased the profit eventually sent to Amnesty—and staff from a local Christian bookshop set up their bookstall. Large copies of the completed crossword blanks were pinned up for checking.

Adults' Questions

5 Across — Thursday of the Last Supper
14 Down — Surname of the traitor
2 Down — Capture in the garden on the Mount of . . .
12 Down — Severed by Peter's sword
18 Across — The charge against Jesus in the Court of the High Priest
17 Down — The régime under which he was sentenced
13 Across — The Governor's symbolic capitulation to public opinion
6 Down — Revolutionary released instead of Jesus
1 Across — Brutal preliminary to crucifixion
15 Down — Place of origin of the man who assisted with the Cross
7 Across — Site of the crucifixion
3 Down — Drug in the wine Jesus refused
19 Down — 'We may not know, we cannot tell what . . .'
21 Across — Traditional abbreviation of the charge nailed to the Cross
11 Across — 'Mother, there is your . . .'
23 Across — Object of 11 Across
16 Across — 'Today you shall be with me in . . .'
22 Across — '. . . Lama Sabachthani'
8 Down — Damage to the Temple Veil
20 Down — He . . . that we might be forgiven
25 Across — Turin's relic of the Passion
9 Across — Ugandan Archbishop who followed the way of the cross in 1977
24 Across — Canterbury martyr
10 Down — First word of the Society which aids prisoners of conscience
4 Down — 'Breathe on me, Breath of God, Fill me with life . . .'

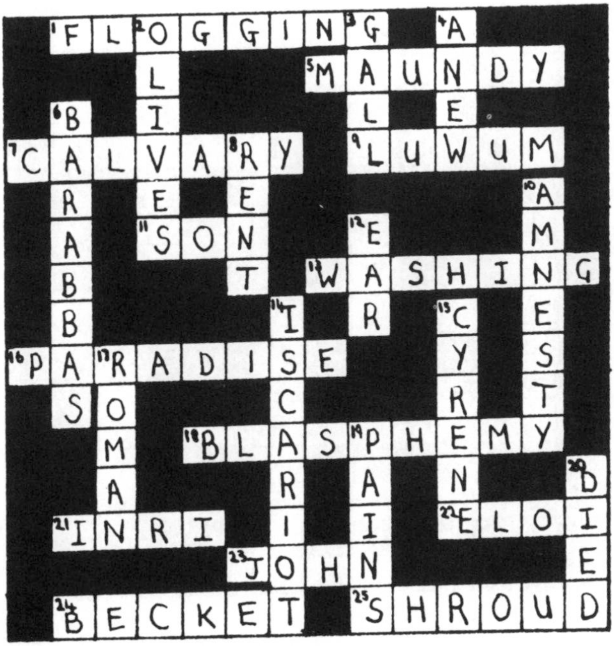

Teenagers' Questions

11 Down	Jesus died during an important Jewish festival
17 Across & 10 Across	During a last meal with his friends, Jesus said that some food would represent his . . . . and some drink his . . .
1 Across	After the meal, they went to a garden outside the city walls
4 Down	Hebrew word for Father, now Pop
5 Across	Number of silver pieces paid to the man who betrayed Jesus
6 Across	The High Priest who presided at Jesus' trial by the Jewish Court
13 Across	Name of Roman Governor who pronounced the death sentence
7 Down	His death was no accident, there was a . . .
8 Down	Stranger who helped to carry Jesus' Cross
20 Across	What did Jesus ask God to do to the Soldiers who nailed him?
5 Down	Number of Crosses on Golgotha
12 Down	The feeling and the darkness as he died
9 Across	Where was he pierced?
19 Across	'Truly this man was the Son of God'—Speaker?
16 Down	The man with a new grave near the site of the crucifixion
15 Down	Woman of Magdala
2 Down	State of the Easter Grave
14 Across	'Now is the Victor's Triumph . . .'
18 Across	Noun for a person who dies for his faith
3 Down	American Baptist Minister murdered for championing Negro rights

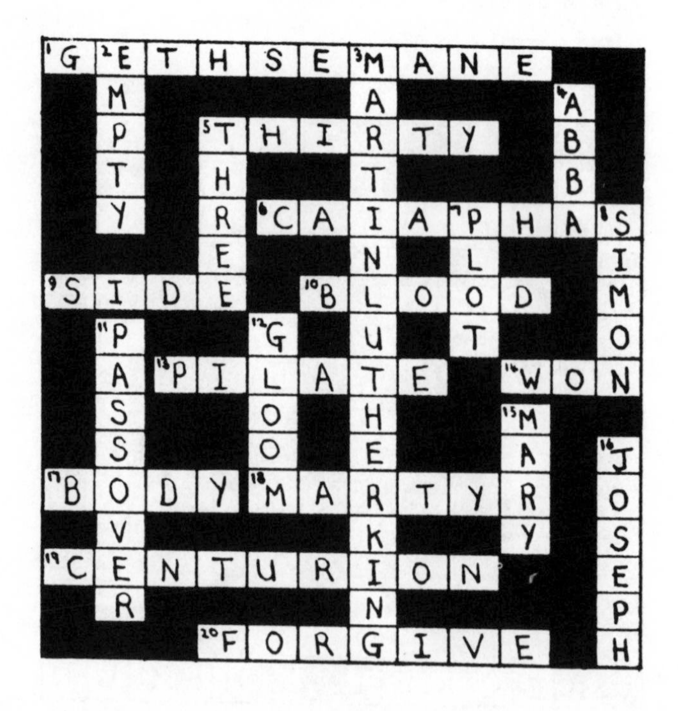

Children's Questions

7 Across	Six days before he was killed, Jesus rode into Jerusalem. What was he riding on?
1 Down & 16 Across	Two items on the menu at the Last Supper Jesus had with his friends
14 Down & 6 Down	Before the meal Jesus . . . his Disciples' . . .
3 Down	What was Jesus doing as he waited for the soldiers outside the City Wall?
16 Down	What were the Disciples told to do?
17 Across	Who led the soldiers to capture Jesus?
8 Across	The secret sign the traitor gave to the soldiers
3 Across	The Disciple who denied Jesus in the Jewish Courtyard
10 Down	Jesus said he was the Son of . . .
4 Across	The King who made fun of Jesus and sent him back to the Governor
2 Down	'The King of love'—but what was he crowned with?
11 Across	Robes worn by Roman Governors
13 Across	How many people were crucified with Jesus?
12 Down	What was the crime of the men crucified with Jesus?
5 Across & 19 Across	As he died, Jesus said 'Father into your . . . I . . . my Spirit'
15 Across	'He died to make us . . .'
9 Down	Door for Jesus' Grave
20 Across	On Easter Day the women found that Jesus' body had . . .
18 Across	On Easter Day Jesus was seen . . .

A PICTURE WALK FOR GOOD FRIDAY

The successor to Ian Robins' Crossword Walk, our previous item

The Picture Walk was organised in the same way as the previous year's Crossword Walk, and again profits were sent to Amnesty International.

Early on Good Friday a small team of men set out along the route with small notices carried on poles; these marked the route and carried a picture of the Passiontide events, in chronological sequence. (Pictures were taken from a number of current illustrated books, principally the booklet of the BBC TV series *Jesus of Nazareth,* published by BBC Publications, and *Our Saviour Lives,* one of a series of 'My Good Shepherd Story Books' published by Concordia. Others—marked 'single picture' on our list—were individual pictures in the author's possession. Postcards or reproductions of works of art could well be used here, or simple drawings in the style of the *Good News Bible,* if there is someone with a skilful pen in the parish.)

In the parish hall where refreshments were served, Bibles were provided for people to check their puzzle answers and there was again a bookstall. When the last walkers had checked out, at about 11.30 a.m., two members of the committee set out to walk round the course, collecting signposts and any litter. Below you will see the sheet given to each competitor, which included blank spaces for him to fill in the picture numbers, here shown completed. Several irrelevant texts were included to make the puzzle harder. These could be omitted.

ON YOUR WALK

You will find 15 pictures telling the story of Good Friday. Each of the pictures fits one of the texts below. CAN YOU SPOT WHICH? Put the picture number beside your choice of quotation, and check your results when you get back to base.

'If anyone wants to be first, he must make himself last of all, and servant of all' (-)

'Behold the man' (9)

'Lift up your heads O ye gates . . . and the King of Glory shall come in' (-)

'Destroy this temple and in three days I will raise it again' (2)

'My Master' (14)

'He gave up his Spirit' (12)
'Rise and pray that you may be spared the test' (6)
'I am the real vine and my Father is the gardener' (-)
'Judas, would you betray the Son of Man with a kiss?' (7)
'Hosanna! blessings on him who comes in the name of the Lord' (1)
'Get up, my child' (-)
'If you have ears to hear, then hear' (-)
'He took bread and gave thanks' (4)
'Father, forgive them, they do not know what they are doing' (11)
'Happy are they who never saw me and yet have found faith' (15)
'He broke it and gave it to the disciples with the words 'Take this and eat, this is my body' (5)
'Do you take me for a bandit?' (-)
'Did you not know that I was bound to be in my Father's house' (-)
'Daughters of Jerusalem, do not weep for me' (10)
'He looked up to heaven, said the blessing, broke the loaves, and gave them to the disciples . . .' (-)
'You do not understand now what I am doing, but one day you will' (3)
'Joseph bought a linen sheet, took him down from the cross and wrapped him in the sheet' (13)
'I shall draw all men to myself when I am lifted up from the earth' (-)
'Are you the King of the Jews?' (8)
'Why search among the dead for one who lives?' (-)
'Surely you know that I have authority to release you and I have authority to crucify you' (-)

Picture List

	Poster no.	Source of picture	Correct text
1.	Palm Sunday	Jesus of Nazareth	John 12.13
2.	Temple cleansing	Jesus of Nazareth	John 2.19
3.	Feet washing	Single picture	John 13.7
4.	Blessing bread	Single picture	Matthew 26.26
5.	Last Supper	Jesus of Nazareth	Luke 22.19
6.	Jesus and Peter in Gethsemane	Jesus of Nazareth	Luke 22.46
7.	Capture of Jesus	Jesus of Nazareth	Luke 22.48

8.	Jesus and Pilate	Jesus of Nazareth	John 18.34
9	Behold the Man!	Jesus of Nazareth	John 19.6
10.	Cross bearing	Jesus of Nazareth	Luke 23.28
11.	Crucifixion	Jesus of Nazareth	Luke 23.34
12.	Crucifixion (close-up)	Jesus of Nazareth	John 19.30
13.	Descent from the Cross	Single picture	Mark 15.46
14.	Mary Magdalene and Jesus	Our Saviour Lives	John 20.16
15.	Thomas and Jesus	Our Saviour Lives	John 20.29

Note: Both this and the Crossword Walk were organised in conjunction with a neighbouring parish and this therefore enabled services to be arranged to complement these more unusual Good Friday programmes: one church held early morning and evening devotional services, the other a traditional Three Hours from noon to 3 p.m.

EASTER TREASURE HUNT

A popular activity with young children who can read, devised by K. L. Cutts

Each clue should be printed on card and pinned in a suitable position in the building where the children meet.

Children need pencils and paper.

Clue 1

Find a sad picture

Of a time of loss.

Who are these standing

Beneath the cross?

[*Somewhere in the room display a suitable picture of the crucifixion; the La Rochette one published by Nelson is very appropriate. Under the picture give the Bible reference St. John 19.25-27. One or two Bibles must be available for reference.*]

Clue 2

The Tomb was the property,

(That's quite clear),

Of a man named J-----,

Of A----------.

St. Luke 23.50-53

Clue 3

A model you can make

I'm sure,

Of the crown which on Friday

Jesus wore.

[*If there is no hawthorn bush growing near the building, the leader should bring some twigs in for the children to use.*]

Clue 4

Will you try to explain the reason

For eating eggs at the Easter season?

The answer lies outside the door,

Beneath a stone upon the floor.

[*In an appropriate place, hide the following verse:-*

In days of old while Lent did last,

People used to pray and fast.

Eggs were not eaten, but stored away

For a special Feast on Easter Day.]

Clue 5

Look in the Gospels

Find St. John

From Chapter Twenty

Copy verse one.

Clue 6

You've nearly finished

Without disaster.

So copy a verse

Of a hymn about Easter.

[*A few copies of the hymn book normally used should be available.*]

Clue 7

On Easter night

When Jesus came to them,

The disciples were staying

In J--------.

St. Luke 24.33

Clue 8

A time to be happy is Easter, when

Jesus rose to life again.

We say it in church when we join in the Creed,

Which is what we all believe indeed.

In the Communion Book find the Creed we say

And copy the words about Easter Day.

[*Have ready a few copies of the Communion Book used in your church*]

There might perhaps be a cream-filled Easter egg for the winner and a small chocolate egg for all those taking part.

LENT AND EASTERTIDE IN MELANESIA

To hear about familiar Christian celebrations held amid the unfamiliar customs of other countries can have a broadening effect—children in your own group may be able to contribute some. Here is a starter from Mary Standley.

'Shall we put the bell in a parcel after Compline, Father?' This strange question was put to my husband by a schoolboy on a Shrove Tuesday on a small Pacific island. This same bell was used to summon the 'boys' (some were young men) to church and to school each day, but during Lent it had to be muffled.

The next morning came the first experience for my husband, small son and me of the Penitential season spent living in the Christian community of the Anglican Mission's Senior Boys' School at Pawa on Ugi—once known as the 'Eton of the South Pacific'. At the Communion Service the palm crosses, made the previous year by the boys from the local sago-palm trees, were burned on Ash Wednesday and the period of self-denial began.

Lent for the Islander is quite different from any other time of the year. In England it can mean less chocolates or cigarettes and more church services, but in scattered, inaccessible islands there are no sweets or cigarettes, so that to talk of 'giving up' things is almost ludicrous. The only real way to teach self-denial there was to have a visible share in the Cross and Passion of Christ. So, as Christ toiled up the hill of Calvary, every Friday in Lent the schoolboys and staff toiled up the school hill (or Jacob's Ladder—a steep set of steps up the hill-side) carrying huge sacks of coral for the station paths, or big boulders on their shoulders to rebuild the wharf which was constantly being washed away by rough seas. All this in the sweltering tropical afternoon sun. This was followed by Stations of the Cross in the Chapel, beautifully and reverently sung in procession.

The boys worked hard all week—school in the morning, farming and other essential jobs for the running of the almost self-sufficient station in the afternoon, Prep in the evening—so Friday afternoon was the great time for Soccer on the two school pitches. Thus, in Lent, as darkness came by 6 p.m., they had little time for their favourite relaxation. On Thursdays a party of boys went fishing to provide their main Friday meal.

The Melanesian had little or no money to give to the church, but he could give his work and time so that the actual running of the church cost almost nothing. Altar breads were made and baked by the boys and incense was procured from a certain tree at Alangaula (where there was a Junior Boys' School to which my husband was Chaplain). The boys cared for the vestments and church linen and prepared all for the daily services. There was no musical instrument, so boys took turns in being Cantor to start off the hymns or psalms.

Maundy Thursday Communion was followed by a vigil throughout the day and night. Two schoolboys kept watch; it was most moving to see the boys—always more than the two—kneeling quietly with their candles and kerosene lamps in the darkness of the chapel and the stillness of the night. Good Friday dawned and we had an hour's Devotion at both schools. After Holy Saturday morning service the boys spent the day in their Bush Houses. During weekends the boys of many different Islands left the school to go up with their own fellow Islanders to the typical homes they had built in the Bush, and fended for themselves. On Saturday evening they came down for Compline and Preparation for Communion.

Easter Day dawned. The long roll of coconut matting, used only at festivals for preservation's sake, was in place down the centre aisle of the church. Flowers were gathered and placed around, and the congregation began to arrive from 5.30 a.m. Pawa schoolboys, Alangaula schoolboys and villagers from all over the Island filled the church to overflowing. Some had been travelling all through the night. There was much reverence and great joy throughout the service and as soon as the Gloria had been sung the bell was unwrapped and rang out across the Island.

After breakfast, everyone made his or her way down to the beach for a big feast, its start at mid-day. Palm leaves were spread under the trees and food was laid out in little banana-leaf parcels all along them. One of our station cows had been killed and cooked, many fish had been caught, cassava and banana puddings had been baked all through the night in a Melanesian oven of hot stones by the shore.

After everyone had eaten as much as they could, there was singing and dancing and then the usual Soccer match between the two schools and any visitors who could make up a team, or a ship's crew if one happened to be in harbour. At 5.30 p.m. the church was filled again for Evensong when the Alleluias rang from the church on the hill top. Darkness gathered then and the villagers began their long journey home—all taking a few parcels of food which had been left over. From the Headmaster's house where we lived on the hilltop near the church, we could see lights from the hurricane lamps bobbing about far and wide. The full moon shone over the glistening sea, the boys returned to their Bush houses for the next day's holiday, and all was quiet save for the cicadas and occasional screech of a parrot or flap of flying foxes' wings. We made a cup of tea on our primus stove and went to bed.